THE BIRTHPLACE OF NEW SCOTLAND

AN ILLUSTRATED HISTORY OF PICTOU COUNTY, CANADA'S CRADLE OF INDUSTRY

Judith Hoegg Ryan

To Anne,
I hope you will enjoy this "visit" back home.

Best wishes,
Judith Hoegg Ryan
December, 1995

A Carolyn MacGregor Book

Formac Publishing Company Limited

Halifax

The development and pre-publication work on this project was funded in part by the Canada/Nova Scotia Cooperation Agreement on Cultural Development. Formac Publishing Company Limited acknowledges the support of the Canada Council and the Nova Scotia Department of Education and Culture in the development of writing and publishing in Canada.

Canadian Cataloguing in Publication Data

Ryan, Judith Hoegg.

    The birthplace of New Scotland

    Includes bibliographical references.

    ISBN 0-88780-292-3 (pbk.)

1. Pictou (N.S.: County) — History. 2. Industries — Nova Scotia — Pictou (County) I. Title.

FC2345.P6R92 1995 971.6'13 C95-950279-3 F1039.P6R92 1995

Published by
Formac Publishing Company Limited
5502 Atlantic Street
Halifax NS B3H 1G4

Printed and bound in Canada.

To my daughter, Ariana

CONTENTS

Preface

Perhaps it was the seventeen years I spent outside of Nova Scotia that awakened my deep appreciation of my birthplace. I am a native of Stellarton, and although I do not live year-round in Pictou County I have nurtured my bond with the area through family, through my enthusiasm for coal mining history, and through regular sojourns to my cabin on Caribou Island. Certainly, I love the area's peaceful beauty, and I am an ardent student of its heritage. So I was excited when Carolyn MacGregor and James Lorimer of Formac presented the opportunity to compile a visual history of Pictou County and, as I made my way through the daunting abundance of literature and set out on the wide-ranging hunt for visual material, I quickly learned that a comprehensive history of Pictou County really merited a set of encyclopedias. In one volume I have been able to accomplish no more than a representative overview of the events and patriots that shaped the area.

The most vibrant period in the county's history was between 1867 and 1918 when a significant industrial economy evolved. This represents the core of the Pictou County story. Choosing what to include in these pages was driven by the industrial history and its impact on the society, it was shaped by the visuals and documentary material available and, throughout, inspired by my wish to make this book very accessible and entertaining to everyone.

To achieve the latter, I was fortunate to find several diaries and memoirs, which are valuable for reflecting the sentiments and culture of their times. Also flavourful in imparting quaint language and ways were early newspapers and magazines, like *Our Dominion* (1887), and *The Eastern Chronicle*. I chose to include little-known details that throw some light on how ordinary Pictonians lived and thought, and on their everyday achievements, not just the big events. Whenever feasible I have identified photos. Although I strived for accuracy, old materials are often faded and frayed, like memories, and I can only apologize for any errors and omissions. Also, I could include only a sampling of politicians,

sports heroes, and other notables, so some readers may be disappointed not to find in these pages people and events they think worthy of mention.

The most rewarding part of preparing this book has been my association with many wonderful people. As I sought both documentary and illustrative material I have been overwhelmed by the enthusiastic response of friends and strangers alike. In particular, locating and borrowing more than 500 images meant imposing on the good will of many people.

As well as sharing their books and postcards, Dr. Howard and Elsie Locke enthusiastically offered ideas and referrals. Michael Sinclair unreservedly loaned his family's photos, along with the memoirs of John MacKay, Caroline Carmichael, and John Sinclair. Clifford MacPherson was his usual magnanimous self with his treasured photo collection. As always, I appreciated the wisdom of Catherine Clark and Evengeline Way. Other friends whose help reinforced what is special about Pictonians were Kezia Matheson, Ida Lawrence, Eleanor Fraser, Patricia Fraser Allen, Jean and Eric Williams, Sheila Robson, Lois Tower, June and John Thompson, Mabel and Doug Sinnis, Clarence Porter, and Murray Holley.

To the many previous strangers who shared visuals or information with me, I also say a heartfelt thank you, and hope that I can now count you among my friends. I appreciate the help of: William MacEachern, who was so generous with his time; Don MacIssac, Raymond Gregory, and J.B. Ferguson whose contributions brought Pictou's past to life; Ted (Chesley) Fraser of Hopewell, for the chuckles as well as the photos; Margaret MacLean's hospitality at Barry's Mills; Josephine Gould of Pictou Landing; Henry and Mrs. Hayman of Westville; Ella Sangster of River John; Margaret Dickie MacDonald of Garden of Eden; Kim Hayden of Blue Mountain; John Soosar; Miller Tibbetts; Cameron and Virginia Garrett; Sadie Barr Brown; Dave Neima; Ella Smith; and, Robert Chambers. I would like to especially recognize the kindness of Haligonian Ken MacDonald, whose Pictou County

Town of Pictou, 1822

pate the challenges; not so, new arrivals. One such woman "gazed through the partially open roof at the waving tree-tops overshadowing them, and within at her shivering little ones clinging round her, and thought of the comforts she had left behind in the old land, [and] declared her wish to be back in Scotland, if it were even to be in a jail."[12]

People lived mostly near the water, in bark-roofed houses of log grouted with moss, heated by an open fire-place. Furniture and dishes were roughly sculpted from wood, while mattresses were made of straw. Most people dressed in cloth spun from their own wool or flax and walked barefoot or in rawhide moccasins. Their few live-stock were primarily sheep. In 1786, government records identify 230 oxen, 356 cows, 450 cattle, 1,500 sheep, and maybe 5 horses in the county. John Gerrond, a Scottish poet who visited Pictou in 1798, noted "wheat, barley, oats, rye, Indian corn, and very fine potatoes," and rivers full of salmon, trout, and eels.[13]

Hand-milling with querns was so arduous that they often did without bread. Money was rare; they bartered their farm products with the merchant and visiting boats.

Despite their travails, the "people were remarkably healthy and vigorous… and, in the country, consumption was almost unknown," remarked Rev. James MacGregor, who arrived from Scotland in 1786.[14]

John MacKay recalled: "Living was comparatively cheap, both as regards food and clothing, the latter consisting chiefly of home-spuns for men and women's dresses."[15]

Snow lasted from November to April with rare thaws. Mildew and smut were common threats to wheat, a princi-pal crop. "Potatoes were the staff of life and they were used at all meals, three times a day. Potatoes and pork were the principle [sic] food. Fish was also plentiful and cheap. A barrel of the largest and fattest mackeral could be had for 20 shillings. Tea was very little used, its price was about 12 shillings a pound. It came down to 7 shillings and 6 pence, and remained so until the monopoly of the tea-trade was taken over from the East India Company. The late James Carmichael was the first merchant settled at New Glasgow, and the only one who sold groceries on the south and east side of Pictou Harbour; yet he was in business for years before he could retail *one chest* of tea in twelve months."[16]

Developing the new colony *To 1827*

Most early settlers lived in isolation, far from the few services available. Paths between inhabited areas were at best a "blaze" — a chip axed out of the trees. Without a compass, when the blaze was lost or hidden by deep snow, a person could travel in circles among perils of swamps and swollen rivers. As John MacKay described it, "The East River was certainly wild enough. The side of New Glasgow, with the exception of a small log shantie at the bank of the river, was then a perfect wilderness inhabited by bears, foxes and rabbits. There were no highways, no bridges, no communication between place and place except by paths through the woods marked by canoes and boats in the summer, and by the ice in the winter. There were but few horses, no wheeled carriages of any sort and only one saddle in the whole settlement. The late Donald MacLellan was its happy owner, and he could scarcely call it his own, for at every marriage Donald MacLellan's saddle was sure to be requisitioned. All works generally done by horses and carts were then performed by oxen and sleds."[17]

By 1807, a ferry was running between Pictou and Fisher's Grant (Pictou Landing). Gradually, roads were driven between settlements. An Act of the Legislature decreed that after snow-falls those with sleds and oxen were to plow. In 1792, the lieutenant-governor announced with great fanfare the beginning of the Great Pictou Road from Halifax, but not until 1813 was it good enough for the mail to be transported by horse. Before then, Stewart, the first postman, used to trudge on foot to and from Halifax, carrying all the mail in his waistcoat pocket, and a bag of oatmeal for sustenance. Beginning in 1816, Pictonians could travel to Halifax by either carriage or sleigh, a journey that took at least two days.

Building the economy

Once they had built their homes and planted their land, the settlers could forge a self-sustaining community out of the rugged, resource-rich land. To acquire necessities from abroad, they started a small trade in timber, fish and furs. Buildings were first erected in downtown Pictou around 1790.

When John MacKay arrived, "there was nothing at Pictou that could, with any propriety, be called a town.

On the Great Pictou Road to Halifax, 1818.
Above: *Blanchard's Hotel, West River.*
Below: *From the summit of Mount Thom.*

There was one blacksmith shop, one tavern and two or three small grocery shops. There was no church, no court house, no jail but a small dingy old log house which was known by the designation of 'The Prison.' Edward Mortimer had his establishment at what was then known as Mortimer's Point, now as 'Norway House.'"[18]

Businesses included Lowden's salt house and store, a carpenter and a ship carpenter shop, John Dawson's house, store and wharf, John Patterson's store, and John McKay's blacksmith's shop. These businesses had strategically located to participate in the growing commerce in Pictou Harbour; although sometimes the tide came right over the road, swamping houses, fishing wharves and stores.

When men like Squire Patterson and Edward Mortimer lifted their eyes under the lofty trees, they must have seen the riches to be made, which would pay for

Lowden's Saw and Grist Mill, Pictou, 1817

imported commodities to sell to the settlers. They could make their fortunes at the same time as building a new economy. So when war with France created a boom in timber exports to Britain, they encouraged eager settlers to cut as much timber as they could. From 1800 until 1820, the timber trade averaged £100,000 annually. Moreover, local wood was used to make ships to carry the exports. The county's first schooner was the *Ann,* built at Merigomish for John Patterson. Captain Lowden, the "father of shipbuilding," built vessels for sale in Britain. In 1798, when his 600-ton *Harriet* was launched, it was the largest to date built in Nova Scotia.[19]

At New Glasgow, James Carmichael started the timber trade in 1809; before long he had expanded into farm produce and opened a store. A blacksmith, a tailor and other merchants moved in, and the town flourished after a rich coalfield was developed near Stellarton.

Who actually discovered coal is a contentious issue, but we do know that as early as 1798 it warmed the hearth of Rev. James MacGregor at Irishtown (Plymouth), and that the family of John MacKay, who obtained a mining licence in 1807, had long known of the mineral. Mining the "Big Seam" (Foord), MacKay raised coal by horse gin and shipped it downriver. The

collier exported so much coal to the Halifax garrison during the war with France that he was encouraged to expand his operations. When coal prices fell after the war, he found himself contemplating his bankruptcy behind the bars of debtor's prison.

Trade with Britain was so good during the wars with France that people acted without foresight. When war ended in 1815, markets declined, and all who had spent or invested imprudently suffered. The "artificial prosperity" particularly ruined farmers. Initially they did well, for their produce commanded high prices. However, seduced by easy money for timber, many neglected their land. Impatient for wood, they cut carelessly, leaving stumps, while over-cultivating robbed farm fields of fertility. Then two natural disasters beset them.

In 1815, the "year of the mice," rodents overran their fields, devouring seeds, crops and grains, fouling maple syrup troughs and attacking small animals. In the fall, the mice died of hunger, leaving a putrid mess both on land and in the sea, "forming a ridge like seaweed along the edge of the sea, and codfish were caught off the coast with carcasses in their maws."[20] Next, "the year without a summer" saw snow in June, ice in July and August and as a result food was scarce and expensive. To exist, many farmers were forced into debt with the merchants and did not recover their losses quickly.

Moral authority

Just as business-oriented individuals took charge to build wealth, men of stature in the fledgling colony assumed the mantle of moral authority until they could put in place legal and social institutions. Philo Antiquarius wrote in the *Colonial Standard* in 1830: "Pictou might be viewed as one family, where the children were all under the immediate superintendence of a good parent. One venerable settler had heretofore presided over the others, advising them to discharge their various duties, and impressing upon them the necessity of honesty, unanimity and industry, while they, with confidence, looked to him as their best director, and yielded in most cases obedience to his counsels."[21] So Philo Antiquarius described Squire Patterson, who was soon joined by *Hector* passenger "Deacon" John Patterson as a leader. "Men took the Scriptural mode of settling disputes....These two old patriarchs...famed as they were for integrity and sound sense, became the general peacemakers."

Another influential figure was Rev. James MacGregor, the first permanent minister in the colony. People worshipped together without a minister, except when one visited, until he arrived from Scotland in 1786. "When I looked round the shores of the harbour, I was greatly...cast down, for there was scarcely anything to be seen but woods growing down to the water's edge. Here and there a mean timber hut was visible in a small clearing, which appeared no bigger than a garden, compared to the woods. Nowhere could I see two houses without some wood between them."[22]

When he arrived at Squire Patterson's house to deliver his first sermon, he was even more disappointed with his parishoners: "as if they had never heard of the Sabbath...[there was] loud talking and laughing, and singing and whistling." Although they listened quietly during the service, afterwards he heard some say, "Come, let us go to the grog shop." Next Sunday he preached up the East River. Again, he found the congregation "disorderly." Undaunted, the selfless man set about his ministry. Summer and winter, he traversed the rugged land, baptizing and teaching the Bible, dependent on his poor flock for inadequate food and a bed on a cold floor. What meagre pay he received went to free slaves in America.

MacGregor's commitment was rewarded when his congregation came to practise and live their religion. Preaching in Gaelic and English, he served the first

The first church was erected in 1787 at Loch Broom (replica shown).

Presbyterian communion to 130 faithful, at an interval on Middle River in 1788. The first churches were built of log: two in 1787 at Loch Broom and on the East River near Duff Cemetery, and one in 1791 at Grant's Lake.

In 1795, the church was bolstered by Rev. Duncan Ross's arrival from Scotland. He was followed in 1803 by Rev. Thomas McCulloch who conducted services in sheds, homes and even McGeorge's tavern, until his church was completed. McCulloch soon became an influential voice in the province, even engaging in a written debate with the Roman Catholic bishop.

The second Bible society in British North America started at Pictou in 1813. By 1815, Presbyterian clergy were also serving at River John and Merigomish.

Most settlers adhered to the Church of Scotland — the Kirk — although the first ministers to come over were Seceders. However, these clergy did not refer to distinctions which separated the Church in Scotland, and the people were content to hear the gospel. In 1817, the Presbyterian Church of Nova Scotia united the congregations and held their first synod in Pictou. However, later immigrants of the Church of Scotland faith wanted their own ministers.

The first Kirk minister to stay in the county, Donald A. Fraser, settled in 1817 among the forty families at McLellan's Mountain, where a church was erected the following year. Fraser preached also at Fraser's Mountain. In 1824, Rev. Kenneth MacKenzie instigated a Kirk ministry at St. Andrew's Church in Pictou.

Early schooling

After James Davidson moved away in 1776 there was no school in the area. Books were scarce. The Dumfriesshire Scots brought some religious literature. Later, John Patterson imported books, including a children's primer. By 1786, many families owned copies of the Bible, though most couldn't read. Occasionally settlers would pool funds to pay a teacher for the few months that children weren't needed for farm work. With such a scattered populaton, many had no schooling whatsoever.

The first of young John MacKay's schools "was with a little Irishman named Patrick Dowling who taught on Fraser's Mountain for a winter….Dilworth's Spelling book, Dilworth's Arithmetic and the Bible were the text books….It was not an easy matter to get hold of anything worth reading….Next winter I attended a school kept by one Andrew Blair, where New Glasgow is now….My next school was kept at New Glasgow by the late James Crerar,…a good teacher, a good scholar, but very short-tempered….Later I attended a school at Irishtown, kept by Angus MacPhie." Later, MacKay himself taught for a period of eight years. He particularly enjoyed his work on McLellan's Mountain where "I was entirely my own master, no other care or trouble; every spare hour in the woods with my gun, or at Sutherland's River with the fishing rod." Over his life he read all he could, claiming the literature influential in his education to be histories of Scotland, England, America, Europe, Greece and Rome, the Encyclopedia of France and Russia, and "Guthrie's Geography [a large work containing sketches and statistics of every country in the world then known]." He also read moral philosophy and the physical sciences.[23]

The sacred old tree, Bridgeville, where Rev. James MacGregor first preached in the upper East River area.

The town of Pictou had schools off and on from 1793 until Thomas McCulloch opened Pictou Academy in 1817 and became the first principal.

Although it imparted a college education, the academy didn't confer degrees and so avoided conflict with powerful Church of England elites, who, as members of the Legislative Council, controlled the educational pursestrings. The boys studied Greek and Hebrew, logic, moral philosophy and natural philosophy. Ministers-in-training advanced to theology. In 1824, the academy released the first seven graduates from Canada's first Presbyterian theological school.

Politics, from revolution to representation

Politics became an issue in Pictou county soon after the *Hector* immigrants arrived and found themselves caught up in controversy over the American Revolution. While they favoured Britain, most *Betsey* settlers supported the Colonies, even naming their children Adams, Burke and George Washington. When they refused to swear the Oath of Allegiance, bitter feelings arose. Some worked against Britain, including a local spy who helped the Colonies capture a Quebec-bound vessel wintering in ice at Merigomish. When the crew of a timber ship at Pictou was lured away to enable an armed party to steal the boat, the American sympathizer who engineered the plot was forced to relocate.

After the revolution, people turned to local issues. In 1792 Pictou was set apart from Colchester district, with its own lower courts. Early sittings dealt with roaming livestock, impounding cattle and regulating the salmon fishery. Killing a bear earned a 20-shilling fine. Later, to finance roads, a poll tax, usually paid in grains or maple sugar, was levied on everyone over sixteen years old, various livestock and every 100 acres of land.

In 1804 stocks were ordered built at Pictou and Merigomish. A courthouse was erected in 1813. Until 1824 the Court of Common Pleas was presided over by community men of stature. A Commissioner's Court dealt with cases of debt. Although the first murder trial before the Supreme Court resulted in a sentence of execution, the convict was spared in honour of George III's Jubilee. In 1819, however, Donald Campbell swung from gallows erected on his father's land, retribution for murdering his parents.

According to historian Patterson: "Trials were not so tedious then. Lawyers as well as judges acted as gentlemen."[24]

In 1799, the Legislature was comprised of a Crown-appointed lieutenant-governor, the governor's chosen council of 12, and an elected Assembly. The members met for up to twelve weeks in winter to investigate public accounts, allocate funds to works such as roads, bridges, agriculture and fisheries, and make laws that were mostly local in application. The unsalaried Council touted themselves as an important middle branch between the Crown and the people but in practice they served primarily for their own interests. As part of the Halifax constituency, Pictou had been represented by members from that city who were of "Loyalist stock." According to historian George Patterson, the "majority... were Tories and high churchmen [who] tended to strengthen the hands of power, and repress everything like popular influence."[25]

The 1799 election was a turning point — three of four candidates for the Halifax seats, including Pictou's Edward Mortimer, were elected on a platform of Reform. These were the days of open ballot, when only men voted, naming their choice aloud in front of all and sundry. Passions ran high; supporters of each side hurled rocks, sticks, rotten produce and eggs at their political opposites. Scuffles and gang attacks were exacerbated by quantities of free-flowing rum. Reformer Mortimer, however, continued to be elected until his death in 1819.

Frolicks

Reform and advancement were becoming evident in other areas of society. Under the auspices of the West River Farming Society, the first plowing match in the province

Pictou Academy

was held in 1818, farm tools and Ayrshire cattle were imported, and prizes were awarded at livestock shows and for clearing land.

In 1822, a subscription library was formed in Pictou. The Weir Durham printing press, donated to the Presbyterian synod, was put to good use at Pictou Academy.

In contrast to enlightenment, the county was "the worst morally that Pictou has seen before or since."[26] Rum had been pouring in from the West Indies since 1794. By 1800, taverns at Pictou, West River and Merigomish, were quenching the public thirst, while "Mrs. G." was entertaining at "a house of bad fame" in Pictou. The timber trade brought "a large influx of population of a very loose character," who "proved most injurious to the social habits and moral condition of the community," like the two young "immoral and scandalous" men bound over to keep the peace

because of "getting drunk, cursing, blaspheming the name of God, fighting and insulting sober people."[27]

Labourers often drank all day as they worked on the docks or at construction and continued to imbibe when they moved into rough lumber camps in the woods for the winter. Author Rev. Patterson wrote that living away from the "humanizing influence of civilized society tends to brutalize men; while the exposure to cold and wet, particularly in river driving, forms a strong temptation to hard drinking, and tends to break down the strongest constitution."[28] Through over-imbibing, some lumbermen would be in debt to their employer by spring, even though each received two drinks a day as part of their wages.

John MacKay grieved the effects of rum on rural life. "A good deal of a farmer's work was carried on by what was termed 'Frolicks', that is, a number of neighbours turned out to do a day's work for another neighbour. This was not a bad way, for the work then to be performed by the farmer was much heavier than his work now, and could not be done by weak hands: such as rolling, burning, and clearing the land. The greatest evil connected with Frolicks was the large quantities of intoxicating liquor drunk at them — and also at weddings — some five, six, seven or eight gallons at each wedding. Never-

Rev. Thomas McCulloch
Below: *Sherbrooke Cottage, Rev. McCulloch's home at Pictou, built in 1806 and here occupied by the E. L. Armstrong family, ca.1900. The roof was later raised. Today the heritage house, part of the Nova Scotia Museum system, is a centre for genealogical research.*

the-less *[sic]* there were not (in proportion to the population) nearly as many drunken persons then as now. Then every person took his glass, from the ministers downward, yet…I was 20 before I saw a man really drunk. It was fashionable to have liquor in every house and to drink it at all times; but it was *not* fashionable to be drunk. That was deemed to be disgraceful."[29]

Writing in 1880, MacKay observed: "People were undoubtedly more sociable 60 years ago than now. During the long winter nights the young people would often meet in some neighbour's house for some hours, perhaps till nine o'clock … singing songs, telling stories, dancing or playing some harmless games. Next night they would meet at some other neighbour's house, and thus a spirit of kindness and good-will was cherished.

"There was more clannishness and rivalry among the people then than now. The men of the East River felt themselves bound to maintain the glory of the East River against all the neighbours and the rest of the world. So did the people of Merigomish, Little Harbour, Fisher's Grant, Pictou, West and Middle Rivers feel bound to uphold the honours of their respective counties against all gainsayers. This sort of clannishness and separation was the source of much fighting and bullying. Each clan or section had its bullies and its courts and militia ministers. These would have their fights. These sectional distinctions were maintained to a ridiculous and mischievous extent; but they all died out long ago."

Clannishness, yes, but for the common good, the plucky people of Pictou County were astute enough to rise above such rivalries. Over the next decades their co-operation would be reflected itself in progressive growth and innovative achievements.

Norway House (shown ca.1900), home of Edward Mortimer. Today the Oddfellows Home.

Edward Mortimer, a native of Banffshire, Scotland, started doing business at his stores and wharves at Pictou after 1788. Timber was his main commodity, but he also dealt in regular and seal fishery products in an enterprise that reached west to Bay Verte and across the Northumberland Strait to Prince Edward Island. Although some of his methods could be "considered unfair," Patterson called him "a born leader of men" and "of first-rate business capacity."

Mortimer's tombstone reads "the poor man's friend." He liked to act "the Lord bountiful" and, while he was generous with credit, that also kept people indebted to him. Mortimer married Sarah, the daughter of Squire Patterson, at that time the most influential man in town. Although Mortimer "rapidly accumulated a large fortune" through his businesses, he died insolvent in 1819, probably because of the decline in trade and because "almost every inhabitant of the county [was] on his books."[30]

Mortimer also served as a justice of the county, a trustee of Pictou Academy, "Chief Magistrate of Pictou"  *for many years, and president of the Pictou Agricultural Society.*

CHAPTER 2

The cradle of industry

1827-1867

Through hard labour and sacrifice, settlers at Pictou had managed to create a civilized life in the wilderness. Over the years, from 1827 to 1867, they built on this base, both economically and culturally. Following the 1825-26 depression in Britain, which produced major setbacks for the timber trade and shipbuilding industry, the county was also confronting poor crops and declining fish stocks. Then the British-owned General Mining Association (GMA) arrived to develop a major industry which would shape the future of Pictou County for well over a hundred years. Their application of steam to coal mining, and to rail and water transportation, established the county as a leader in technology.

Pictou Harbour

River John

In fact, Pictonians enjoyed their first train ride three years before Queen Victoria did in England, the home of the railroad. In Pictou harbour, the new steamships bobbed at anchor side-by-side with impressive schooners, launched from county shipyards, from River John to Merigomish. This was the period when Pictonians asserted themselves internationally, as their sailing vessels, captained by local skippers, plied the oceans.

Meanwhile, small manufacturers were setting up using local resources such as clay and limestone, while tradesmen and mills began to free people from the manual home labour of cloth-making, querning flour, and building furniture. Though much farm work was still onerous, rural neighbours now had time to help each other with big tasks.

As more immigrants arrived and the region developed into a centre of commerce and industry, Pictonians led the battle for reform in politics and education. Religion diversified, as other faiths formed congregations alongside Presbyterianism, which meanwhile maintained its influence, even exporting missionaries to the other side of the world. With prosperity and stability, Pictonians began to indulge in a variety of cultural and recreational activities.

By 1867, Pictou County was truly linked to the rest of the continent by railway and by politics as a part of the new country of Canada.

Steaming towards the future

In 1827, businesses in Pictou were working to address the decline in their economy wrought by the depression in Britain. As timber prices plunged, merchants no longer carried credit for their customers — farmers, sawmill operators, labourers — while they waited for the market to turn around. Shipbuilding was almost eliminated, another result of depressed markets. In addition, agriculture was severely hit by wheat fly and potato disease. Gradually, however, the timber trade came back, though it was reduced by overharvest to mostly spruce and birch products: the majestic trees of fifty years before were gone forever. Although similar poor stewardship had brought a downturn in the fishery, the reciprocal traffic of Pictou fish for West Indian sugar and rum survived. Throughout,

The Samson

In August 1833, the Quebec-built Royal William *steamed out of Pictou on her way to claiming fame as the first boat to cross the Atlantic using steam alone. At a cost of £17, 10 shillings, a ticket bought "splendid accommodations" for the historic voyage.*

the coal mines were experiencing ups and downs, small operators producing merely 3,000 tons by 1826.

So the future looked less than auspicious when in 1827 Frederick, Duke of York, granted the General Mining Association (GMA) of England a sixty-year lease on minerals in Nova Scotia. Although the GMA didn't find precious metals, they did prospect a mineral that promised to bring wealth to the company and the region. In the age of the steam engine, coal was a key to prosperity. While Pictou's pioneer coal mines had been rudimentary, the GMA sailed into Pictou Harbour fortified with knowledge of the latest mining techniques and carrying modern machinery, as well as engineers and skilled colliers. As they set to building Albion Mines, they were laying the groundwork for heavy industry in Canada.

Within three months the Storr pits were producing coal. By December, the first steam engine built in Nova Scotia had replaced horses for pumping and hoisting. The GMA dug limonite from riverbanks near Springville, then smelted the yellowish-brown iron ore in their own blast furnace. The *Richard Smith,* launched from Fisher's Grant in 1830, was the first steamboat built in

the province. An impressed Joseph Howe wrote in 1830 that £70,000 had already been spent at Albion Mines, where the GMA directly employed 130 men and gave much work to local tradesmen and coal carriers.

A horse tramway transported coal one-quarter mile to a wharf on the East River. The GMA extended this road, replacing wooden rails with "fish belly" iron rails cast in their foundry. The standard gauge split-switch road was ahead of its time. Eventually, increased output necessitated the construction of the Albion Railroad. Although Peter Crerar, a teacher and road surveyor, had never laid eyes on a railroad he proved to be capable of surveying, engineering and supervising the building of the acclaimed new six-mile line to Abercrombie, where coal chutes and a 1500-foot wharf facilitated loading to large vessels.

Three "iron horses" arrived in parts at Pictou, accompanied by their English engineer, fireman and brakeman.

The *Samson, Hercules* and *John Buddle* were assembled by W. H. Davies, a blacksmith who had come over with the GMA. These became the first locomotives to run over iron rails in Canada, and were also the first six-coupled (three pairs of driving wheels) on the continent. Great fanfare marked the opening of the Albion Railroad on September 19, 1839. Amid feasting, dancing and torch-light parades, 3,000 excited Pictonians rode the rails for the very first time.

The coal line offered the first passenger service in the province. Three trips rolled daily into Abercrombie, where the *Pluto* waited to ferry folks to Pictou. The harbour had been enjoying the progress of coal-fuelled steam naviga-tion since 1831, first with the *Richard Smith,* and later with the GMA's SS *Pocahontas* and SS *Cape Breton,* which traded with Northumberland Strait ports. Passengers on the four-hour run to Charlottetown paid twelve shillings for a cabin. Until the turn of the century, packets and ferries left Pictou for other Maritime ports, while larger schooners employed in worldwide commerce also called Pictou home. From 1834, the coun-ty's first lighthouse, at Cole Point, beamed mariners to safe harbour.

In 1840, Pictou became port of registry for ships built along the north shore. Shipbuilding was revived, partly to accommodate the Maritime trade but also to sell ships. However, many vessels were thrown together with inferior materials and workmanship to make a quick profit. After a few years' boom and a rapid decline, some shipbuilders and entre-preneurs started building superior ships to serve the flourishing trade in fish and timber. Captain George MacKenzie, a renowned shipbuilder, launched ships at Boat Harbour, Pictou and River John, which he then captained. From 1840, he built at the James Carmichael yard in New Glasgow.

By 1835, the industry was well established in River John. Several vessels weighing over 500 tons were built dur-ing the next half-century, many in yards owned by the MacKenzie and the Kitchen families. At 762 tons, the *Nashwaak* was the largest. In the Merigomish area, more than fifty ships were built. All timber used — except imported hard pine — was local, and the sails came from the sail loft in Pictou.

Captain George MacKenzie launched his 1400-ton Hamilton Campbell Kidston, *which he skippered up the Clyde River into Glasgow where no big ship had ever dared go before.[1] Captain MacKenzie's 1465-ton* Magna Charta *held the record for size for many years.*

McPherson's Mills Grist Mill, now restored, was built by William McPherson in 1861. For more than a century it processed grains from surrounding farms, and served as a community centre, housing a post office, barber shop and store.

The wealth of the land

In 1837, sadder but wiser landowners gathered at the Royal Oak Tavern to form the Pictou Agricultural Society, which helped organize rural agricultural fairs. In 1838, James Fraser sold the first cultivator in the county, imported from Boston. In 1840, author George Patterson's father introduced a threshing machine which worked on a tread-mill principle. Two years later, Thomas Blaikie of Green Hill submitted a request for a patent for an improved threshing machine. One of his references stated he saw Blaikie "with one horse thresh 24 sheaves of oats in the space of one minute and a half…and… caused the oats so threshed to be cleaned and measured." Another attested: "One great advantage in the machine… consists in it being easily and without the least injury carried from barn to barn where it occupies a very small space — the propelling part of the machinery remaining on the outside."[2] Through advancements in cultivation and animal husbandry, farmers came to produce better goods and to eventually prosper, bringing an end to their dependence on the merchants' credit system.

The "House of Hamilton" exported throughout Eastern Canada and to the West Indies.

To process wool, the first water-powered carding machine was erected at Middle River in 1822. Seven years later, the first fulling and dyeing mill, near Durham, moved to Six Mile Brook. The first spinning machine and power loom was set up near Springville by a member of the Grant family, who also had a furniture factory and carriage shops. Saw and grist mills were built along several rivers. So much grain was ground locally that G. J. Hamilton's opened a biscuit factory in Pictou in 1840.

At Irishtown Rev. James MacGregor was reputed to have the first house made with bricks manufactured by the GMA. Ireland-native Mitchell Burns operated a pottery for sixteen years in Parkdale. In 1867, the Crown Brick and Pottery Company was processing clay around McLellan's Brook. A platter at the Nova Scotia Museum labelled "the Nova Scotia Pottery Company, New Glasgow, 1869," suggests other clay works were in operation.

Small industries developed out of the abundance of natural resources. Springville lime was used at Albion Mines, while Robert MacNeil sold his Quarry Island grindstones as far away as the United States. On January 30, 1856, the first cast was made in the Pictou Iron Foundry, where the *James Primrose* was built — the first engine in

Pictou to use steam power for manufacturing. Smaller manufacturers included Ross's Soap and Candle Factory and Pictou's John Geddie, Clockmaker.

Rail connections

Significant progress came in land transportation. In 1828, for £2 you could leave Halifax on the Eastern Stage at 7 a.m. Tuesday, and arrive at Pictou the next evening at 8 p.m. Weekly coach service to Antigonish started five years later. Although "comfort and security" were advertised, the rough roads were rutted and muddy. Carriages rolled through pitch black night often guided by no more than a single lantern. Road improvements throughout the province were ongoing. Once the road over Mount Thom was completed in 1842, Hiram Hyde started a daily Pictou-Halifax service of 14-18 hours' duration, picking up passengers at Nancy Stewart's house on Mount Thom. Hyde also built a telegraph line from Truro to Pictou in 1850. Roads out of New Glasgow were opened around Fraser's Mountain in 1847 and to Antigonish via the Marshy Hope Valley four years later.

In 1858, the Nova Scotia Railway lines from Halifax to Windsor and to Truro were completed. On November 30, 1864, the ground was broken at Fisher's Grant — the terminus for the railway's Pictou extension. The line would pass through Albion Mines and New Glasgow, as well as have access to deep water shipping at the terminus. The project was soon in disarray as patronage seeped into the awarding of contracts. Sandford Fleming, the supervising engineer, uncovered a significant amount of incompetence, indifference and larceny. Contracting to build the line himself within time and budget, he paid off or discharged almost all the contractors. For this, he was pilloried and caricatured in a partisan press. Fleming displayed both a singularity of purpose and engineering innovations that set the standard by which future railway projects were judged. Among his achievements were a superior roadbed and tunnels, instead of bridges, wherever possible. The two large iron bridges he did build were widely acclaimed, particularly the East River Bridge between Stellarton and New Glasgow with four 79-foot spans. He used the first steel rail in the area. By May 31, 1867, the entire 52 miles were operating, with several stations along the way. Fisher's Grant Roundhouse had stalls for six locomotives and an enclosed turntable. Among the accolades from famous railway builders was "the only railway in America in which all the works of art are entirely of permanent materials, either iron or stone."[3]

The railway was important for social and economic reasons. Although by now Nova Scotia had roads, land transport was a long, interrupted coach trip, while sea travel was often harsh and circuitous. By train one could visit relatives and see the country efficiently, comfortably and inexpensively.

The railway was now an integral part of society in PIctou County and played an important role in the area's economic growth. Employment expanded the regional administrative headquarters of New Glasgow and Stellarton. Mining expanded to supply the demands of coal-burning steam locomotives. The railroad opened up inland areas to the products of local mines, forests and farms, prompting the industries to expand. At the same time, it also brought from further away competitive products, breaking down Pictou County's isolation and autonomy.

Two cultures, two futures

1827–1867

Displacing the Mi'kmaq

As the economy progressed, settlement correspondingly expanded through increased immigration. But these developments had a very negative effect on the native peoples. The Mi'kmaqs lost all control of the land and their lifestyle, already shattered by disease and alcohol, was further degenerated by government policy. Although they were granted hunting and occupancy rights on south-east Pictou Harbour and around Merigomish, the land was not "reserve", so they were gradually pushed out as settlers moved in. They were forced into dependency, yet given only meagre provisions, such as blankets and a kind of coarse blue cloth, known as Indian cloth. Silas Rand remarked, "An old Indian said to me…that they could spread down the skins of the bear and moose, and cover themselves with others, and in the severest weather would be warm and comfortable anywhere.

'But,' said the Indian, '…our lands have been taken away, the forests have been cut down and the moose and

A Mi'kmaq family at Pictou Landing

Paintings of, top, *Pictou Landing;* middle, *Pictou Harbour;* and bottom, *grazing sheep, by William Hind.*

Hannah Carmichael (Mrs. Issac) Matheson

Presbyterian ministers

the bear nearly exterminated. We have no skins to wrap ourselves up in winter. Government, it is true, gives us a bit of a blanket, and we spread it over the children. One awakes crying with the cold, and gives it a pull; and then another awakes crying, and he gives it a pull; and by 'n by, they pull 'em all to pieces.'"[4]

In 1828, an Indian Civilization Society was formed in Pictou, aiming to teach Mi'kmaq children to read and women to spin and knit. The society failed, Mi'kmaqs having no desire to embrace European society. Indeed, they were appalled by European manners. "Their own children are taught to respect their parents," noted Rand. "Many a white man could learn from them in this respect."

A Mi'kmaq helping Rand translate the New Testament commented that the Scottish could take lessons on courtesy and humility from Luke 14, verses 7-11 when they visited the camps. "They think us about on a level with beasts, but we speak of their ignorance and ill manners among ourselves....In reality, an Indian thinks as much of his camp, as the Governor does of his palace."[5]

Patterson wrote, "When we consider the unfeeling manner in which they have often been treated, it is wonderful that they have been so quiet and free from deeds of violence...."[6]

He commended Mi'kmaq honesty in not stealing livestock or farm tools as their own lands and means of support were taken away. They were forced to hoe potatoes — although not naturally farmers — chop wood, sell fish, make buckets and baskets, and even to beg in order not to starve. They still loved to shoot moose or spear salmon, but those traditional pursuits were now rare. Although Patterson was among the very few to rue the bad treatment of the Mi'kmaq, his declaration reflects paternalism rather than outrage that a free and autonomous people had lost everything that was ancestrally theirs — their land and unfettered rights over it, as well as their liberty to live as they liked.

Hardly threatening to the settlement were Mi'kmaq festivities, and it did permit an annual gathering. In September more than 100 canoes from Antigonish, Prince

Along the East River

Edward Island and Pictou would be paddled to Fraser's Point or Middle River Point, where the Mi'kmaqs enjoyed two days of games, feasting, singing and praying. After 1838, they moved the festivities to Indian Island, Merigomish.

Among the celebrated Mi'kmaqs of this time were Patlass, an expert at draughts, and Lulan, a former warrior, who claimed to have scalped 99 persons, as well as rescue John Patterson when he fell through ice.

Building town and country

In 1827, the county's population of 14,000 was almost all of Scottish descent. Between 1827 and 1848 the GMA brought more than 300 miners from mining areas of Great Britain to Pictou County. Ships continued unloading Scots at Pictou, and in the 1840s came destitute Irish, forced from their homeland when the potato crop failed. Patterson remarked that Pictou County actually suffered some out-migration of young people to Australia, men to California, and women to domestic service in New England, a practice that was common up to World War II.

When Joseph Howe visited the county in 1830, he wrote that Pictou town had a population of 1,500 and between 150 and 200 buildings, "including some very handsome private dwelling Houses, and some large and commodious stores....

Its wharves stretch into the Harbour....The ride around the Harbour of Pictou is very pleasant....Above the town, on the side and brow of the Hill, are numerous cleared fields, gardens and pasture lots, which add to the beauty of the water view of Pictou....The waters of the broad Harbour are spread out like a bright mirror before the eye; bounded on the left by the high land which stretches away towards McLellan's Mount, Merrigomish, &c and on the right by the woodland that lies between Pictou and the River John; while the East, West, and Middle Rivers, the folds of which are lost in the foliage of the trees and the undulations and the irregularities of the land through which they flow, seem, as they wind away from the opposite shore of the harbour, like vast and beautiful veins, passing through the very heart of the country — the happy medium of circulation for the animating and sustaining tributes of Agriculture, Manufactures, and Commerce." [7]

Howe was also impressed with Albion Mines, where he stayed overnight "snug and safe at Mount Rundle," the GMA superintendent's manor house that was set in a large park and was famous for elegant entertaining. The company operated "an extensive store, cellar, counting house, &c, in which are kept a more various and extensive stock of goods than is to be found in any mercantile Establishment in the country. This store is intended for the supply of the persons more immediately engaged about the mines, and is also a great convenience to the population on the East River, who resort to it for supplies which, from the facilities for purchase and importation the company possess, they are enabled to furnish upon the most advantageous terms."

By 1838, Albion Mines boasted 250 wood and brick miners' houses, a comfortable inn and a tavern.

Many villages were busier then than today. Howe called Bailey's Brook "a very thriving and pretty Highland settlement."[8] Merigomish enjoyed shipbuilding and the timber trade. Springville had mills, quarries and farms, while Durham was a centre for the timber trade with several general businesses and licensed inns. In 1849, Durham Post Office ranked fifth in the province in revenues collected, one place below Pictou. A sure sign of a growing rural area was the opening of postal routes.

Both men and women worked hard on the land and in the home. Gradually, though, they turned to tradesmen and businesses for commodities which they had previously had to produce themselves. In the country, frolics continued to be the favoured method of completing large tasks such as plowing and stumping. While the men worked the women prepared large quantities of food. After the work was completed they held a "spree" with fiddling, dancing and singing. Unwed women often worked as domestics or as cooks at mills during busy seasons. Others went out to homes, dressmaking for the day.

When shopping meant a wagon trip to town, two or three neighbours travelled together. A typical shopping list from 1855 reads, "28 lb. sugar, 3 lb. tea, 1/2 bushel salt, 2 gallons codfish oil, 5 lb. nails, rice, hair oil, pills, some rum, one coil fiddle strings, one box Holloway's Pills, one pot of ointment."[9]

Adversity regularly struck in the form of forest or grass fires that burned down homes and barns. Weather was a limiting factor in rural life; heavy snow and bad roads meant confinement. Ongoing good health was a challenge, if mill owner James Barry is any example. In his diary, while only in his 30s, he regularly complains of debilitating ailments such as toothache, colds lasting months, unidentified stomach upsets and boils. He treated them with assorted self-prescribed remedies: "I am now

Sailboat between Pictou and Pictou Landing

using Dr. Geo. B. Green's Oxygenated Bitters, I think they are good for the stomach. I used to think that purging was to work wonders for the stomach, but, by golly now the more I use of them, the weaker my stomach got [sic]. I am now dead against heavy and continual purging. Occasional [sic] it may be of use…I have myself to blame for having this cold. I bought some 'cotton flannel' and got it made into shirts, and put off any 'woolen flannel' and put on the cotton flannel which cheated me completely. All the time I wore the cotton flannel I had a touch of the cold."[10]

Patent medicines accomplishing any number of miracles were advertised. Mountain Herb pills, from the mountains and valleys of Mexico cured all afflictions, especially biliousness, impure blood and worms. Mr. Winslow's Soothing Syrup conquered everything from teething to "griping in the bowels." J. W. Jackson in New Glasgow sold the celebrated Rogers remedies for cancers, tumours, ringworm, corns and warts. Females in delicate health were being exhorted to travel to Boston to see the celebrated Dr. Dow, who was also expert in dealing with seminal weakness and the degenerative effects of boys having engaged in "a secret and solitary habit." Birth control was hardly an issue, if the claim to fame of Mrs. Murdock of the Ponds, Merigomish was any example. In December 1866 she became the mother of her "second seventh son," after having already had seven sons, one daughter, then six more sons.[11]

Virulent diseases brought by immigrants and sailors also struck the county at various times. A lazaretto was built in Pictou in 1848, where the infectious could be quarantined. Regardless, an epidemic ensued in 1852, after the barque *Tongataboo* sailed into port carrying smallpox-infected passengers. When the sick were put ashore at Abercrombie, local people found out and complained. The diseased were ordered back on the ship, but one man escaped to a sailor's boarding house in Pictou, where he spread the smallpox.

By 1866, the county comprised three busy towns and several villages. Pictou was both a busy port and a seat of learning. Albion Mines hummed with entrepreneurship after the GMA lost their monopoly in 1858, while New Glasgow continued to enjoy commercial and industrial growth stemming from the coal industry.

Institutions to bond and to build

1827–1867

The politics of reform

Throughout this period, Pictou was becoming a well-established area with a mix of rural and town folk. Politics, religion and education were intertwined, as ongoing areas of controversy. In ridiculing the schism between the Secessionists and the Church of Scotland, a split that reflected itself in politics, culture and particularly education, Joseph Howe commented in 1830, "Barbarous…dirty-phiz'd radicals and red-headed Highlanders [engaged in] degrading and paltry bickers…abode of patriots and den of radicalism — where the spirit of party sits, nursing her wrath to keep it warm, during ten months of the year, in order to disturb the Legislature all the other two.… It is impossible to live on the fence; or in fact to live at all, without 'going the whole Hog' with one of the

The Pictou Courthouse

parties into which its society is divided. The Lord only knows whether we may ever live to go out, but here we go merrily in — we may be burned by the AntiBurghers, or eaten without salt by the Highlanders."[12] The debate was led from Pictou town by a coterie of well-educated Scottish immigrants and graduates of Pictou Academy.

In 1826, the permanent funding for Pictou Academy was defeated by the Council and the annual grant was withheld until 1831. The academy, a liberal arts college that also trained men for the Presbyterian ministry, was opposed by both Anglican Nova Scotians and the Church of Scotland because the theology taught was Secessionist. The Kirk wanted the academy to teach the basics of grammar school instead of higher education. Principal McCulloch was kept busy lobbying, writing and travelling in attempts to defend the institution.

Another vocal ally of the Academy was the first Pictou newspaper, the *Colonial Patriot*. On December 7, 1827, the day the first steam engine in Nova Scotia started up, so did the first newspaper outside of Halifax. The *Colonial Patriot's* editor was lawyer Jotham Blanchard, a graduate of the first class at the academy. The newspaper provided an ideal organ to advance the various points-of-view in the conflicts arising in church and state.

As well as politics and opinion, the first issue discussed in the newspaper was the importance of size and location of cows' barnyards, advocating that organic material be laid down so that the movement of cows would compost it. There was a section on government affairs in Canada, and a religious treatise on the Israelites' descent into Egypt. Although an editorial denounced drunkenness as "the crying sin of the present…and a cruel highwayman," on the next page, D. Crichton & Son advertised: "Just received from the Caribbean, a quantity of rum, sugar and molasses." James Skinner offered "fine cloths, handkerchiefs, knives and forks, quills, paper, tobacco, snuff, powder, starch, sole leather, etc." For sale at Pictou was a house that rented for £15 a year and a large house with a store owned by James Dawson. Two properties in Merigomish were up for sheriff's sale. Roads Commissioner Peter Crerar was calling for tenders for two bridges in the county.

Condolences were expressed to the family of Mr. Arthur, who, commanding a ship owned by Mr. Taylor of Pictou, was washed overboard in the West Indies, and to the widow and eight children lamenting the death of Little Harbour farmer James Reid, whose boat was upset. Robert Lander, a Sunday school teacher and "an ornament of the Provincial character" was also drowned. The last page featured poetry and some amusing tales of daily events.

Blanchard used his publication to fight for reform. The Council of 12 wielded power that was arbitrary and self-serving and they regularly overturned decisions of the House of Assembly, while the governor acquiesced. Although this new liberal newspaper claimed loyalty to the King and the British Constitution, its editor believed the best way of showing this was in advancing the interests of His subjects. Like the Reformers in Britain, Blanchard was keenly interested in the subject of popular rights. He had no compunction about "calling public functionaries to account, and to hint that tax gatherers and smuggler seizers may not be immaculate in official duties, and infallible in legislative conduct," wrote Patterson in his history of the county. "Jotham Blanchard was the first public man in the province, by voice and pen to press for Responsible Government."[13]

Jotham Blanchard

Originally scathing, Joseph Howe vigorously debated with Blanchard in the press, but Howe was converted to Reform and successfully led the struggle for Responsible Government. To counter Blanchard's attacks, the government party established the *Pictou Observer* in 1831, and the two newspapers engaged in lively debate.

Blanchard was elected to the House of Assembly in 1830 in a contest so violent that a man was killed. Local controversies such as Pictou Academy and the Presbyterian split influenced the vote. Although Blanchard and three other popular candidates were returned, the whole Assembly proved ineffectual against the Council. In 1836 Pictou was legislated a separate county, with two

representatives for the county and one for Pictou township. Over time the county elected representatives from both the Reform and Tory parties. In 1847, Reform won a majority of seats in the province and the next year succeeded in taking office. George Young was the county's first cabinet minister. In the late 1850s, Reformers took the name Liberal; Tories became Conservatives.

On July 1, 1867, Premier Charles Tupper brought Nova Scotia into Confederation. Three Pictou County Conservative MLAs voted for the union, while the fourth — James Fraser — did not. That Confederation was not popular in the province was evidenced in the overwhelming election of Liberals in the next provincial election, including four from Pictou. Nova Scotia also sent Liberals to the first federal Parliament. New Glasgow merchant and shipbuilder James Carmichael won locally. Under Joseph Howe, the anti-confederates went to Ottawa with the intention of taking Nova Scotia out of Confederation, but Howe was eventually induced to stay, and the issue was grudgingly put to temporary rest.

The Academy

The most contentious issue for Pictou at the time of Blanchard's election was Pictou Academy, which a grudgingly respectful Joseph Howe visited on July 7, 1830: "Shall we take a peek in? After all the hot blood it has created, and all the hot words it has occasioned, a man might well be excused for pausing upon the threshold of the place — for who knows but the very air of it might be impregnated with the spirit of discord." Howe described a wooden two-storey building with a belfry, surrounded by poplar trees, with a laboratory and a classroom on the ground floor, the museum and a library upstairs. The lab boasted "philosophical apparatus" for natural science, including "bottles containing chemical compounds ranged on the shelves....The library is extensive and well-chosen....But the museum offers the richest treat that can be had within the Province — containing, as it does, an ornithological collection embracing nearly all the birds of the country, from the stately loon to the beautiful chick-a-dee." Howe waxed poetic about "the Mottled owl...the beautiful blue-winged duck, choice object of epicurean care...the saucy sea pigeon...Robin

Prince Street Prebyterian Church Choir, 1865. Standing: *Lizzie Smith, Annie Curry, Laura Campbell, James Hepburn, Robert McConnell, William Matheson, William Johnston.* Seated: *Maggie Johnston, Maggie Wilson, Sarah Smith, Mary Ann Harris, Susan Campbell, Clarence Primrose, James McKinlay, John Parks.* Below: *Emily Matheson, Clara Ross.*

Red Breast, the pleasant harbinger of spring….Gladly would we allow each bird in this beautiful collection to lend its wing to our spirit, and carry it back to some happy hour of our bygone days — our rapturous recollections." He called Thomas McCulloch's museum "honorable to the Academy and the province." Indeed, McCulloch entertained John James Audubon in 1833, who extolled his natural history collection.[14]

Unable to get money for the academy out of Halifax, Blanchard sailed to London for support. The British government instructed the governor to grant the school a permanent stipend and to settle the differences surrounding the school. In resolution, the divinity training was moved out, and the old grammar school crammed into the academy with the upper classes. Decline in the quality of education led to the school closing for two years. Though never a college, the Academy gained fame for excellence. Under the Free School Act, it became a county academy in 1865, preparing students for university. In 1838, Thomas McCulloch was transferred to Dalhousie College as principal. He died five years later, at age 66. He is credited with being one of the most outstanding characters in the history of education in Nova Scotia.

Among Pictou Academy's graduates, according to

McPhie's *Pictonians At Home and Abroad,* were eight college presidents. Geologist Sir John William Dawson was born in Pictou in 1820. After graduating from Pictou Academy and then the University of Edinburgh, he was hired to lead a geological survey of the coal fields. Under his tenure as the first Superintendent of Education for Nova Scotia, the Normal College opened in Truro. In 1855, he was appointed principal of McGill University. Knighted in 1884, Dawson continued to write, so that by the time he died in 1899, his bibliography of papers, pamphlets and books numbered 551 titles on such subjects as coal formation, reptile discoveries in Nova Scotia and the Bible.

Other graduates include Rev. George M. Grant, born in Stellarton, principal of Queen's University in 1877; Rev. Daniel Gordon of Pictou who succeeded Grant as president of Queen's; Rev. George Patterson who is remembered primarily for his invaluable histories of Pictou and other counties; and J.D.B. Fraser, the first physician to use chloroform during childbirth in Canada. Among the academy's female graduates, one finds Scotsburn native Anna Elizabeth MacLeod, who graduated from Dalhousie in 1906 "with great distinction" then went on to become principal of the Protestant Schools of Antigonish, as well as Mary and Jemima MacKenzie of

Waterside, who graduated from Dalhousie Medical School, and went on to establish missions in India.

Religion

By the time Rev. James MacGregor died in 1830, his pioneer ministry had grown to encompass six separate congregations, while Pictou had become home to the Presbyterian synod and divinity school. Over the next decades, more parishes were established and Presbyterianism remained a church divided in two. In 1843, a split occurred in Scotland in the Kirk when some clergy broke away to form the Free Church. Several Kirk ministers in Nova Scotia moved back to Scotland to replace the deserting ministers, while Rev. John Stewart renounced the Kirk Church of St. Andrews in New Glasgow to form the Free Church, or the Knox Church, taking most of his parishoners with him. With only one Kirk minister left in the county, adherents endured a 10-year wait for new clergy. In 1854, at Sutherland's River, the first church was formed that united Kirk, Free and Nova Scotia Presbyterians. Subsequently, the Presbyterian and the Free churches of Nova Scotia united in 1860.

Until Pictou's St. James's Church was completed in 1827, Anglicans were served by occasional visiting ministers. One of these, Rev. Charles Elliott, settled in as rector of St. James, travelling once a month to River John where St. John's Church was consecrated in 1849. He also travelled to Albion Mines, where in 1851, miners took a day off to erect the frame of Christ Church on land granted by GMA and paid for by popular subscription. A plaque in St. Andrew's Cemetery in Egerton indicates a Roman Catholic congregation there in 1810, while the oldest church in that area, St. Mary's Church, Lismore, dates to 1834. Not until 1828 did a Catholic priest, Rev. Boland, settle in Pictou town. A congregation was added in 1840 at St. Mary's Church in Albion Mines. The first Wesleyan Methodist Society formed in River John in 1822, while adherents of that faith in Albion Mines were served by circuit ministers until one settled there in 1845. Scottish Baptists were in the county early and other Baptists formed their first society in 1838 at Merigomish, although they didn't have a settled minister until after 1874.

The Presbyterian Church in Nova Scotia was the first religious group in any British colony to fund and establish a foreign mission. The clockmaker's son, Rev. John Geddie of Pictou and his wife, Charlotte MacDonald of Antigonish, left in 1846 and travelled over 19,000 miles to Aneityum, New Hebrides, where they spent 24 years. Rev. J. W. Matheson, born in Rogers Hill, settled with his wife in Tanna, New Hebrides, in 1858. Both died after four years there. Over the decades, other Pictonians spread the gospel at missions in the Pacific, the Caribbean, Indochina, China and India.

An enlightened society

School and church provided enlightenment, while newspapers and books provided education and entertainment. Begun in 1832, the *Juvenile Entertainer* was the first paper for young people in the province. The *Eastern Chronicle,* first published in 1843, was an unabashedly Liberal newspaper. It was foiled somewhat by the *Colonial Standard* after 1858, espousing Conservative politics. Within a few years of settling, the GMA provided a school and a library at Albion Mines. In 1835 the Pictou Bee printed the first Gaelic book in the New World. *Companach an Oganaich* ("The Youth's Companion or Pleasing Instructions") was a collection of "Sentences, Divine, Moral, and Entertaining." In 1830, Dawson was advertising the province's only book store outside of Halifax, "Books, Stationery, Catalogues and an Almanack adapted to the Meridian of Pictou." After 1834, the Pictou Literary and Scientific Society presented lectures and held lively discussions, while Springville's Strathbeg Reading Society offered books and speakers to educate its members. Occasionally preachers from various sects or lecturers on current thinking orated their philosophies at public gatherings. Among them was Reverend Barker who lectured to the Pictou Mechanic's Institute in 1866 on "The mind is the man."

Mill-owner James Barry of Six Mile Brook provided a printing and bookbinding service. His personal library contained books on a wide array of religious and philosophical subjects, all topics he liked to debate with

ST. JAMES CHURCH, PICTOU, N.S.
CANADA

The Pictou County Missionaries

One can only marvel at the sureness of faith that would inspire Rev. John Geddie and his wife to travel so far from anything familiar, as their daughter Charlotte wrote, to "go to an island whose inhabitants were heathen of the lowest type, and not within a thousand miles of a civilized community." The "Letters of Charlotte Geddie and Charlotte Geddie Harrison" indicate that when their ship stopped at Fati, New Hebrides, where they'd hoped to set up a mission, they discovered a whole ship's crew had been killed a few months before. The missionaries concluded, after seeking divine guidance, to sail on to Aneityum. There, "a young man who came to live on the mission premises, because he had become a Christian, was seized and killed, and a cannibal feast followed in a grove not far from the house." Another time the house was torched because the Geddies and their colleagues tried to prevent activities such as the strangling of widows immediately after the death of the husband.

Once, trying "to prevent the deed, Mr. Geddie was surrounded by male relatives with lifted clubs, and rendered powerless." When his own life was threatened, the missionary appeared fearless and "at length the perpetrator laid down his club and went away." As well as their insecurity at the hands of the natives, the Geddies endured an earthquake and tidal waves. They returned only once to Pictou. John Geddie died in Australia in 1872. A memorial stone at Aneityum says that when he arrived there were no Christians on the island, but when he left there were no "heathens." Charlotte spent her last years in Melbourne, Australia.

Sir William Dawson called Charlotte "a woman of resource, judgement, and courage, and was most devoted and untiring in her exertions."

While her husband worked to "sell the gospel to the wild, fierce natives of the New Hebrides," she ran a school for women and children and also taught them sewing. She expresses delight in their progress: "I can hardly belive that these respectable looking men and women…are the same naked, degraded looking human beings, whose appearance when I landed…made my heart sink…almost…too low to be reclaimed."

Jemima MacKenzie was the youngest of twelve children of a Waterside family who graduated from Dalhousie Medical School in 1904, placing first in her class in surgery. For thirty-five years she served as a medical missionary in India, where she adopted forty-four children, many of whom had been abandoned because they were girls. Church literature says she "braved wild animals and bandits" in order to spread the Good News.

like-minded friends. Being a fiddler, he was also an avid collector of Scottish music.

Every culture embraces music in some way, so, in Pictou County, Mi'kmaq festivities, the arrival of the *Hector* passengers, wading ashore to the sound of the bagpipes and the refinements of Victorian music have been part of the country's musical mosaic. The first music printed in Nova Scotia was done so by James Dawson at Pictou, in 1836. The *Nova Scotia Songster* was a collection of "Scotch, English, Irish, Love, Naval and Comic Songs," while the *The Harmonican* was a compilation of religious music. A Philharmonic Society established in Pictou in the 1850s was one of several dramatic and musical groups. A miners' band that started at Albion Mines in the 1840s associated with the 78th Pictou Highlanders in 1907, by which time it was made up of talented musicians from the surrounding towns. Over the years this band was led by sons of the musical Mooney family. The 78th band served overseas in World War I as the regimental band of the 85th Batallion and even performed in the 1919 London Victory Parade.

The county was also visited by travelling musicians and performers. Anna Swan, the giantess born just outside Pictou County in New Annan, was exhibited by P. T. Barnum in the Mechanics Hall in 1866. She was the tallest lady in the world, standing 7 feet 6 inches, and weighing 350 pounds. "Everybody should see her," read the recommendation, for an admission fee of 15 cents for adults, 10 cents for children. Other celebrities, including the Prince of Wales in 1860, and his brother Prince Alfred who stayed in style at Mount Rundell, enjoyed visits to the area.

Lodges became popular during the nineteenth century. Masonry didn't really take hold until Albion Lodge was chartered in New Glasgow in 1840. Oddfellows' Eastern Star

Lodge opened in 1854 and the Loyal Orange Lodge took hold in the mining areas. At Durham in 1827, the first Temperance Society in the province (the second in British North America) was formed. In 1830, 73,994 gallons of liquor cleared Pictou customs. To the horror of many, this equalled about 5 gallons for every man, woman and child, at a cost of not less than $4 each. The temperance movement under such names as the Sons of England and Independent Order of Good Templars maintained the fervour. Club outings were popular. At a picnic held by the Refuge Lodge of Temperance at Pine Tree, and described in the *Eastern Chronicle* in August 1866, members were "charmed by the wild music of the Pilbroch." After "regaling themselves of the dainties provided in abundance," the evening concluded with a "tip of the light fantastic to the sweet music of the violin."

Sports became important recreation. The collier towns competed at cricket. Frozen rivers were available in winter for skating, hockey, curling and even horse racing. Pictou celebrated Queen Victoria's coronation in 1837 with a regatta. The boat races became a yearly event and included foot races and games. In the 1850s, New Glasgow obtained a bowling alley, and the Pictou Curling Club was a going concern by 1850.

The *Eastern Chronicle* of August 1866, cited the winner of the provincial Cogswell Cup as an unidentified "Crack Shooter" from New Glasgow. That year Colin F. MacKinnon, a boy from Bailey's Brook, took second prize in the Highland Fling at the Antigonish Scottish Gathering; Daniel Falconer won the Egerton plowing match; Hugh MacDonald and Angus Smith of Fox Brook captured a large bear which yielded 70 pounds of grease; and Capt. D. Fraser scored 18 points to take the medal in the annual firing of the 6th Regiment of Militia at Springville.

On the brink of Confederation, Pictou County was undoubtedly a buoyant, prospering society.

CHAPTER 3

Building Canadian enterprise *1867–1918*

The years between 1867 and 1918 were the most vibrant in Pictou County's history. With the GMA monopoly revoked, new capital moved into the coalfields and development took off at Thorburn, Westville and Stellarton. Coal mining became the driving force in the local economy. Wealth was not without its price, however, as routine death and disaster underground established the long unhappy tradition of miners' blood buying prosperity around them. Two tragic explosions impelled the struggle for pioneering mine safety legislation and a trailblazing miners' union, led out of Stellarton in 1882, fought and won reforms in the working conditions.

Just as Britain and Europe were enjoying an industrial revolution, so innovative Pictonians recognized the potential for economic growth. "We have coal and iron," they reasoned, "why not steel?" And utilizing both local minerals, from steel manufacturing came a subsidiary car plant in 1913, that still produces rail cars for the international market.

Meanwhile steel poured at Trenton spawned many factories putting out a wide range of goods. By 1916 the annual value of manufacturing was $1,273,018 — more than for any other county except Halifax. Whistles calling from various plants were an ongoing reminder of industry at work. Along with steel ships, tools, boilers and bridges, the county prospered through brick-making from local clay, woodworking from

Miners' Monument, Westville, erected 1873 in honour of the sixty explosion victims.

sawmills, and food processing. Carriages, leather, luggage, furniture, glass, cloth — the county produced practically everything needed at home, while exporting goods through an expanding transportation network. By the end of this period, rural and urban residents were debating whether the motor car was here to stay, or merely a nuisance fad. Who would have believed that 100 years before there were barely paths joining the county's isolated farms?

The wealth of enterprise attracted newcomers looking for work. As most settled near their jobs, four industrial towns and the shiretown, Pictou, expanded to serve them. Shopkeepers promised an array of goods from near and abroad, while financial and other business services offered consultation about insuring a house in a new subdivision or investing in a factory. Classy hotels catered to a steady stream of "drummers", enticed by the growing market for commercial goods.

Adding to the air of exhilaration was the advent of new technology that revolutionized people's lives. The telephone made the world smaller, while electricity made it brighter. Pictonians shrugged off their Victorian smugness to embrace new opportunities with vigour and ingenuity, such as building an electric tramcar to move people among the upriver towns.

The need for social institutions was vigorously addressed in modern hospitals and progressive schooling, while new churches reflected a broadening of religious belief. Maintaining the commitment to social well-being, the county elected free-thinking politicians to provincial and federal governments, where many served in the Cabinets. As Pictonians built their community, a cohesive, unique identity was evolving, an identity fostered by

ACADIA WORKS

WESTVILLE, N.S.

Published for W. A. Reid, Westville, N.S. 2422

enthusiastic social interaction. Uplifted by the boom times around them, they danced, sang, made music and drama. Friendly rivalry was evidenced between sports teams, many of them champions, while recreational pursuits like skating allowed folks to get to know one another. Excursions and picnics were fine-weather entertainment enjoyed by neighbours and lodge kin. Sharp-eyed investors saw the opportunity afforded by more leisure time and pay envelopes to introduce motion pictures and travelling shows to the theatres and music halls. By 1914 the county saw itself as mature; the youthful county of 1866 had been propelled by a heady brew of energy, foresight and optimism and was now part of the mainstream economy.

Mines and men

After 1867, the economy of Pictou County evolved from its natural resource base to a vertical structure of new industries. The energy that fired this industrial boom was coal. As well-capitalised speculators moved in and sank modern mines, large tonnages of fuel became available. The expansion began in 1866, when Black Diamond, Acadia and Intercolonial all sank mines not far from the muddy Gairloch Road. As the companies built housing and laid railways to Pictou Harbour, Acadia Mine — renamed Westville — was born. Likewise, in 1872 the Vale Company sank the Six-Foot and McBean Mines, developing the community christened Thorburn in 1886.

Drummond pityard

Albion Mine

On April 2, 1914, several outside workers had taken shelter from the bitter cold to eat their lunch in the warm boiler room at the Drummond. They were sitting directly above No. 5 boiler when it suddenly blew up, violently killing seven men and creating devastation.

Meanwhile, at Albion Mines — now called Stellarton in honour of a seam of oil-coal which burned like shooting stars — the GMA had moved out, selling their Cage and Foord Pits to the Halifax Company. In 1880, Halifax sank the Albion and MacGregor, two mines that would put out coal for 75 years. Mining expanded, resulting in a merger, in 1886, of the Halifax Company with Vale and Acadia to form the Acadia Coal Company. Henceforth, Acadia Coal dominated the industry in Pictou County, although throughout the years other companies operated.

In 1904, the mayors of Stellarton and New Glasgow turned the sod for Acadia's new mine in the Foord seam, which had lain seductively thick and untapped since the Foord Pit exploded in 1880. Like its predecessor, the Allan Mine was in the vanguard of engineering and technology and was designed to produce 1,000 tons of coal a day. A thermal plant alongside would make electricity. The new Allan mine symbolized optimism for a future of coal-fuelled prosperity, which was reflected in a total output for Pictou County of 700,000 tons in 1913.

Despite the rich resource, mining was not easy. Due

to excessive methane, fires and explosions had destroyed several pits and taken many lives. Experts considered the gassy Foord seam to be the most treacherous in the world. Other coal veins in Stellarton and Westville were almost as bad. It was not only explosions that made the mines hazardous. The men faced hazards such as runaway coal trips, gas inhalation, clashes with tools, and falls of coal and rock from rotten roofs.

The hopes and dreams of the many who came to work the coal became tempered by the reality of their dangerous workplace. Peter Barrett, an immigrant from Cornwall, England, wrote in his diary: "I again applied to Mr. W. Blacker of Acadia Coal Mine and he gave me good work....In August following there was an explosion in the mine I worked in; fortunately I was not down at the time, but was on the bank head, and saw the effects of the destructive element of gas. A few men and boys were badly burned, one or more died. We were thrown idle for some time."

In 1873, 60 men and boys died when Westville's Drummond Mine violently erupted. Peter Barrett wrote: "The sight was terrible. I think there were [many] lives lost;

Foord Pit explosion

some were Cornishmen. The shock was felt for miles at the midnight explosion. I do not know if there was [sic] praying men lost in that pit or not....

"Dense volumes of smoke were coming up the slopes of the Drummond Mine, buildings were shattered. The high brick air stack was blown down. We went onto the downcast shaft, which was still clear, some men had been taken up by the horse gin, alive, but badly burnt....I saw Edward Burns, and Abraham Guy, a Cornishman, descend the slope as volunteers....

"It was agreed that Guy should remain down and Burns should come up to tell the state of the pit. The signal was given to wind up, instantly there was a tug of wind up the shaft, then the air reversed, and suddenly the terrible explosion followed, blowing up debris probably hundreds of feet high into the air, carrying away in its fury, the gin, and all the gearing of the shaft head, and as we ran for our lives, the debris fell all around us. Fortunately, no one on the surface was seriously hurt. But

after the blast was over, we found poor Burns dead, about 20 yards from the shaft, frightfully blackened and mangled. The mine was smothered, and flooded, and has since been reopened."[1]

In November 1880, a blast ripped through the state-of-the-art Foord Pit, snuffing the life from 44 miners. Fires blazed for weeks, so that it finally became necessary to enlist the New Glasgow fire department's steam pumper, the *Lulan,* and pump water from the East River into the pit. Another 13 men were blown up in the Vale Colliery in 1885. Fire — often spontaneous — and explosion plagues the Pictou coal industry even until today.

The Foord explosion was a catalyst to calls for improved mine safety. The Provincial Workmen's Association (PWA) — the first all-Canadian craft union — had been founded the previous year at Springhill, under the leadership of Scottish-born newspaperman Robert Drummond. Lodges soon formed at Thorburn, Stellarton, and Westville. Drummond moved to Stellarton in 1882, where he started the *Trades and Labour Journal,* and as Grand Secretary of the PWA, he persisted lobbying until government legislated reforms that led to an improved quality-of-life, both above and below ground. Among the advances came night schools, regular mine inspections, and certification of miners and officials. Early evidence of PWA's power came after an eighteen-week strike in 1887 defeated the company's attempts to reduce wages. The PWA represented most Nova Scotia coal miners until the United Mine Workers of America usurped them in 1919, after a long and bitter struggle.

Birthplace of steel

The "black gold" produced by the blood and toil of colliers became crucial to the prosperity of the whole county. Unquestionably, the most aggressive and revolutionary new enterprise to rely on coal was steel-making — an idea of genius, born out of necessity as, after 1867, the old economic underpinnings of the area began to crumble. The change was evident by 1880, when steel steamships were supplanting wooden schooners, once the pride of the local

Limestone Quarry Workers, Bridgeville area

shipbuilders. At the same time, the protective trade policies imposed after Confederation had eliminated advantages the Maritimes had enjoyed with previous trading partners, particularly the United States. As the sale of products moved inland via the railroad, shipbuilding declined.

Recognizing that the glory days of sail and the mercantile trade were past, far-sighted entrepreneurs saw that they had to employ the available raw materials for manufacturing. Most noteworthy were New Glasgow blacksmiths Forrest MacKay and Graham Fraser, who formed the Hope Iron Works in 1872 to make railway and marine parts; they subsequently started the Nova Scotia Forge Company. The establishment of their Nova Scotia Steel Company at Smelt Brook, north of New Glasgow, was the foundation of Trenton — a small town that can proudly proclaim itself the "birthplace of steel."

The first steel ingots in Canada

Men of Steel:
top, *Graham Fraser;*
bottom, *Forrest MacKay*

were manufactured here in 1883. In 1888, *Our Dominion* boasted of the company: "The only one of their kind in Canada.... Distinctive.... The product is the finest quality of cast steel.... This company manufactures all kinds of steel namely: machinery, spring, tire, toe, calk and other staple grades;...it employs 160; and... trade extends to all portions of the Dominion."[2]

As the first step toward an integrated company, by 1892 MacKay and Fraser's New Glasgow Iron, Coal and Railway Company was mining iron ore around Springville-Bridgeville. At Ferrona (Eureka) they built the first coal wash plant in North America, as well as coke ovens and a blast furnace to produce pig iron. From the Inter-Colonial Railway at Ferrona they laid twelve miles of track along the East River through their iron and limestone quarry areas, terminating at Sunny Brae in 1895. Ore from mines known as Cameron, Black Diamond,

Pot of molten steel at Trenton plant, circa 1900.

MacDonald, Grant, Saddler and Black Rock was processed by about 300 men up until 1904.[3]

When quality ore ran out, the company acquired the lease on iron at Bell Island, Newfoundland, then bought the GMA coal properties at Sydney Mines to smelt Wabana ore. After forming Nova Scotia Steel and Coal (NSSC) in 1900, they built a plant at Sydney Mines, making steel ingots and sank new coal mines there for their integrated operation. Open-hearth steel-making ended at Trenton, and Cape

Because the war had called so many men overseas, women were hired by industry. Although they proved skilled, dedicated workers, women were let go when men returned from overseas.

Breton-made ingots were used instead in their rolling mills and forging plant.

In 1912 the New Glasgow-owned steel company was producing fifty per cent of the steel used in Canada. During World War I no plant in the British Empire, outside of Great Britain, equalled Trenton's production of 14 million forged shells.[4] It also made armour plate used in early pattern tanks, and plate for the hull and boilers, and all of the steel needed by the shipyard in Trenton. At the peak of the war the steelworks employed 2,100 men and women, who travelled by tram and train from all over the county.

Manufacturing for the nation

"No section of the Eastern Provinces is so distinctly industrial as that part of the province, the centre of which is New Glasgow, Stellarton, Westville and Trenton — towns which stand as symbols of an industrial development and expansion… as great as that of any section of the Dominion." These remarks from a promotional publication were in no way hyperbole, for indeed, by 1914 Pictou County was an industrial mosaic.[5]

Capitalizing on local steel production, several enterprises manufactured secondary iron and steel products. I. Matheson & Company, for example, founded their Acadia Foundry in 1867 to specialize in steam engines and boiler making. In 1902, blacksmith J. W. Cumming began forging coal mining tools and equipment. Cumming later bought out Alexander MacPherson's sawmill factory. The company still operates as Maritime Steel and Foundries. John Stewart made the province's first iron bridge, spanning the East River at Springville; his suspension bridge was the first iron crossing of the river at New Glasgow.

Stewart's plows received the highest awards at county and provincial exhibitions from 1879-1884. Another innovator, William Fraser's foundry became known for its Buckeye mowing machine. Two other noted manufacturers were Maritime Bridge and Steel Furnishings.

During World War I, many plants expanded to shell and armament manufacture. The Albion Machine Company set up in the Stellarton rink. Canadian Tool and Specialty was turning out 600 rifle sites per day in a process that required 103 operations. The war further boosted the county's economy when Nova Scotia Steel and Coal launched the cargo vessel *War Wasp* in July 1917, followed by six similar ships. Locks were even built on the East River to accommodate these launchings but were later removed.

More than 1,000 wooden vessels were launched in Pictou County before steel replaced timber. In 1884, the *Warrior,* built and navigated by the Kitchens of River John and weighing over 1,600 tons, was the largest ever of Pictou County's sailing ships. By then only Kitchen and Archibald MacKenzie were building square-riggers at River John. The last to come from the area was the barque *Orquell,* in 1879. After 1875, only nine vessels were launched from New Glasgow including the *James William,* the Carmichael yard's 440-

ton steel schooner. The last schooner launched from New Glasgow was Walter MacNeil's *Annabelle Cameron* in 1918.

Pictou County sawmills turned out a variety of items at this time, including shingles, rakes and ax handles. Wooden furniture was made at Piedmont, and very ornate furniture was made at Abercrombie. A grandaddy armchair came from Hopewell. Garrett's of New Glasgow started importing, upholstering and repairing furniture in 1882, but their claim to fame was patented rug hooks and designs. Garretts of every successive generation showed talent for creating artistic patterns, and the rugs are valuable items today. D. Porter and Son at Stellarton was one of several companies that provided wooden materials for construction, as building kept up with the thriving economy. An ad for D. Fullerton & Sons, Dealers in Lumber, Rough & Dressed, Pictou read: "The planing, sawing and moulding mill of Messrs. D. Fullerton & Son, whose doors, sash, blinds, mouldings, etc. are known throughout the trade radius of Pictou, ranks amongst the most important of the manufacturing industries of this area of the country...with...a large trade throughout NS."[6] Fullerton also manufactured wool carding machines.

By 1876, homespun clothing had been replaced by imported cloth or cloth

In September 1913 the first boxcar rolled out of the Eastern Car Company, which was started at Trenton by NSSC head Thomas Cantley. The NSSC subsidiary made coal cars and train cars, shipping to Russia and France during World War I. Next door, Dominion Wheel Foundries built iron wheels and brake shoes for Eastern Car's products.

milled locally. One local mill, the Kerr Mill at Middle River, was destroyed by fire in 1869.

Despite a large financial loss, according to the *Eastern Chronicle* of July 28, 1883, "with indomitable courage and energy they rebuilt the late mills and...built up a trade that extended over the whole of Nova Scotia and a large portion of New Brunswick."[7] In 1882, Kerr invested "vast expenditure" in refit and expansion. The three-storey wooden structure with four floors handled the complete process from picking to weaving, employing "30 hands" to turn out an average of 200 yards of cloth daily.

On July 18, the mill was "filled with a busy crowd of workmen....Every machine was in active operation, and

The James William. *The* Eastern Chronicle *of July 17, 1908, described the launching of the only steel schooner built in Canada: "Such a crowd watched...no other vessel launched slipped from the ways more gracefully." It was christened by Miss Hannah Matheson, daughter of W. G. Matheson, in charge of I. Matheson. "The sail out the bay was delightful, the day perfect, the water was still as a mill pond." Lemonade, ice cream and cake were served. Premier W. S. Fielding sent congratulations, hoping for a return to the good old days when a ship from New Glasgow was on every sea. The Maple Leaf Band played and the Salvation Army held a service at the square.*

all hands were happy and cheerful as it was well known that the mill would be taxed to its utmost capacity" to fill all its orders. At 10:30 a.m. wool on its way through the "picker" caught alight, and with the current generated by the fast movement of the machine, "immediately the picker room was one seething mass of flames, the rapidity of which can only be realized by those who witnessed the terrible sight....Within ten minutes from the origin of the fire, access to the mill at any point was impossible. Employees hurried to the scene of the alarm being given, but being beaten in their attempt to quench the flames, and driven by the intense heat to the next flat, rushed out....The flames followed them...and to save their lives [they] had to jump through the windows of the second storey."

After fire spread to the store, saw and grist mills, "the dense volumes of smoke that rolled from the doomed buildings, the roar and fierce crackling of the flames proceeding from five burning buildings, the eager, anxious and excited cries of the workmen, friends and neighbours aiding and encouraging each other,...and the terrible march of the destroying flame combined to form an impressive scene." When the dwelling caught fire, eager hands managed to put it out, but 30 or 40 acres of fine-growing timber also burned. By noon all was a "smoldering mass of ruins." The total loss of $30,000 was insured for only $1,000. Miraculously, no one was killed.

Wool was also milled in the busy village of Eureka, until that mill burned down in 1915.

Clay from Sylvester, Meadowville and Westville all found its way to local brick works, but it was Parkdale that became known as "the Pottery." By 1916 Standard Clay of Quebec was producing 52,000 tons of clay products yearly at factories and kilns on 63 acres. The village of Priestville began as a home to many of its workers.

Pictou manufactured almost as much leather as all other counties in Nova Scotia put together, with Logan's Tannery of Lyons Brook pre-eminent until its closure in 1921. Although most shoes were still cobbled, the Pictou Boot and Shoe Company and Stellarton's Fraser Brothers were in the footwear business in the 1890s. *Our Dominion* touts the products of William Chisholm, Jr. of New Glasgow: "This is undoubtedly an age of travel, in which we almost lose the sense of our nationality and become thorough cosmopolitan citizens of the world, travelling rapidly from one country to another. In by-gone generations the family trunk was handed down from father to son, and probably served the purposes of the whole family in the few and intermittent journeys that were then taken. In the present progressive age, when men move rapidly across oceans and continents, a very large field of enterprise is

From 1881–1917 New Glasgow and Trenton were home to the province's only glass works, the products of which are prized by collectors today. By 1884, the Nova Scotia Glass Company's Trenton plant employing 100 workers was lauded for its beautiful diamond flint crystal. The company specialized in embossed tumblers for lodges and special events. The business was bought out by Montreal's Diamond Glass Company, who closed it in 1892. Two years earlier, however, three Lamont brothers began glass manufac-

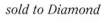

ture, particularly of lamp chimneys for lighthouses and the railway. Although their expert workers produced a superior product, by 1897 high freight rates rendered the Lamonts uncompetitive with larger central Canadian glass companies, and the brothers

sold to Diamond

In 1899, the glass works buildings were destroyed by a spectacular fire, described as follows in the Eastern Chronicle *of August 31, 1899: "As the roofs fell in, myriads of sparks were flung heavenwards, and being driven afar by the wind, died in the upper air, while mingling with the flames of red were columns of blue fire from zinc jar rings melting, and an occasional breath of deadly gas from kegs of arsenic burning. All through the fiercest of the fire a constant sound from the bottles bursting led one to think that a thousand companies of infantry were practising at hand, and when the floors were gone and the walls all laid low, tons and tons of molten glass lay through a good part of the ruins." After losing so much stock, Diamond shut down the Lamont works.*

Since 1890, five Humphreys brothers also had been making a large assortment of glass products. In 1906, their workforce numbered 75, working double shifts to supply manufacturers in the Maritimes and Quebec, including Minard's Linament, who were taking 300,000 bottles at a time. The plant did well until 1917 when the Humphreys relocated to Moncton because of cheap natural gas. High commercial gas rates forced them out of business in 1920 — a disappointing finish to a unique Pictou County industry.

opened up for the manufacture and sale of trunks, valises, and travelling bags in general." Chisholm's were handmade of the best materials, and "no more solid, substantial, and durable trunks are to be obtained on the market."[8]

Also in New Glasgow, James Eastwood employed 20 people, manufacturing and wholesaling jewellery, including articles imported from Europe and Japan. The Francis Drake Company, Manufacturer of Carbonated Beverages, Nerve Food, Choice Fruit Syrups, Steam Factory, was a new business extolled by *Our Dominion*. "When the tendency of the present age is undoubtedly in favour of

temperance drinks... (Drake's) productions have won their way to popularity with wonderful rapidity... lemon, strawberry, raspberry, orange, pineapple, vanilla, and other syrups...Belfast ginger ale in quarts or half pints, also lemonade, sarsaparilla, champagne, cider, soda water. (Their) Standard Nerve Food is highly endorsed by the medical faculty."

Tobacco was not the scourge it is today. In Pictou, A. McKenna carried on "a very important trade in tobacco, and

Brick Works, Drummond Colliery, Westville, N. S.

expanding population. Farmers peddled their products door-to-door; they also supplied the growing number of mills, vegetable canners, butchers, grocers and bakers.

From the 1870s, there were cheese factories at East River, Gairloch and River John. George Vinten's creamery operated in New Glasgow for a few years in the early 1900s, but the real successes in this industry were the co-operative dairies. Through Scotsburn Co-Operative Dairy, begun in 1900, many farmers of the west Pictou area shipped eggs to Halifax, each one imprinted with the farmers' own stamp. At Stellarton, Picoda Dairy opened in 1913 to process the cream from the east of the county.

One of several grist mills, the New Glasgow Milling Company — complete with grain elevators — was strategically located for export on the East River. As well, local

statistics go to prove that the inhabitants of this continent are the largest consumers, in proportion to population, of this fragrant weed. The manufacture of tobacco into cigars, and also into plugs or twists for smoking or chewing, forms a prominent industry and gives employment to a large number of hands... (McKenna) enjoys excellent relations, and handles none but the best imported leaf tobacco. He turns out annually about 40 tons of tobacco."[9] McKenna's Pictou Twist was the chewing tobacco traditionally favoured by coal miners.

Bread and fishes

Significant prosperity derived from harvesting and processing food from both farm and fishery. During the mid-nineteenth century, Pictou farms surpassed all Nova Scotia counties in butter, wheat, and oat production, and did well with other grains, potatoes, and hay. No longer dependent on borrowing a neighbour's saddle, most farmers travelled in comfortable carriages — perhaps purchased from D. Polson, Carriage and Sleigh Manufacturer of New Glasgow. Even when many were leaving farms to take employment in industry, agriculture became progressive and responsive to the needs of the

Oyster and clam harvesting

flour was utilized by bakeries, like Campbell's West Side Bakery with its "Bread of Merit", or Lynch's Limited, whose Stellarton branch advertised in 1915 that it was "equipped with modern machinery which takes the flour from the barrel and passes it on through all the various operations, with the hand scarcely touching the material until baked into bread, thus making the product perfectly sanitary."[10] Their bread was delivered daily to all towns and major villages, and shipped elsewhere in northern Nova Scotia and to Prince Edward Island.

The waters of the Northumberland Strait have also yielded significant food resources. Over time, hard working county fishers have harvested salmon, cod, mackerel, herring, scallops, clams, oysters, and lobsters. To encourage lobstering, the federal government operated a hatchery at Bayview in the 1890s. By then canneries at Black Point, Caribou Island and Pictou Island were regularly shipping to central Canada and England. In 1875,

Scotsburn Co-operative Dairy in its early days.

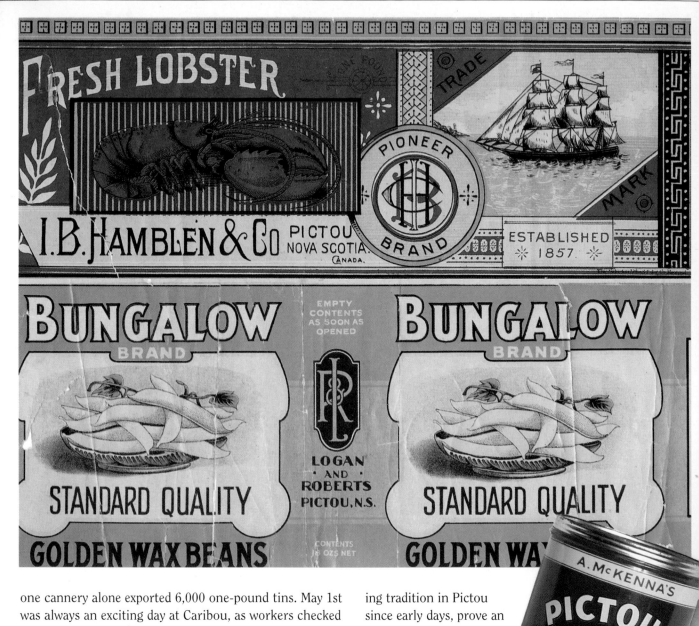

one cannery alone exported 6,000 one-pound tins. May 1st was always an exciting day at Caribou, as workers checked into company boarding houses, like Logan and Murdock's, for the busy May-June season. By World War I the firm of Burnham and Morrill alone had 11 factories along the strait producing one million pounds a year. Although lobsters have been canned all along the coast from River John to Lismore, the most enduring cannery started at River John in 1910. Broidy's became Maritime Packers — a business that grew and prospered until it was bought by National Sea Products 55 years later.[11]

Lobster fishermen worked hard in those days before engines and hauling equipment. Out in their small sailboats before sun-up, they were buffeted by wind and waves as they hand-pulled in two or three tons of lobster a season. Although modern boats and gear have eased the toil, making a living on the sea is still arduous and dangerous work. Annual lobster boat races, which have been an ongoing tradition in Pictou since early days, prove an exhilarating relief and give the fishers the opportunity to showcase their skills.

Travel the modern way
As the business and population expansion demanded improved transportation, Pictou County aggressively availed itself of the most up-to-date means of both local and distance transport.

After Confederation, the railway became the foremost means of travel and trade, making stagecoaches obsolete, except through remote areas. Water travel, too, declined. As early as 1874, the paddlewheeler, the *East Riding*,

Provost Street, New Glasglow

stopped ferrying along the East River, although the *Alexandria* went on carrying passengers and freight down-river to Pictou for several more years.

Several rail lines were built to give northern Nova Scotia access to markets east and west. The Eastern Extension was completed from New Glasgow to the Strait of Canso.

In 1893, the Carmichael yard launched the SS *Mulgrave* to ferry trains across the strait. Built by I. Matheson of New Glasgow, it was the first steel ship constructed in Nova Scotia.

A 15-mile link was opened from Stellarton to Pictou town in 1887, while the "short line" from Brown's Point to Oxford Junction gave the Northumberland shore access to the ICR. By 1912, the 13 passenger trains steaming daily out of Stellarton were a small part of the passenger and freight traffic pasing through the town.

Children put themselves in peril playing on and around trains, while many people were killed walking the iron bridge between Stellarton and New Glasgow, especially in winter when the roads were not cleared. "There's a Red Light on the Track for Boozer Brown" was a popular Salvation Army song that reflected the high incidence of men killed while walking or passing out on the track.

Train wrecks were always very spectacular. The *Eastern Chronicle* of December 8, 1887, carries a headline telling how Locomotive No. 170 was "Blown to Atoms" while standing at Stellarton station. The force of the blast

completely wrecked the engine, throwing parts and crew in all directions. Four men were killed and the station was heavily damaged in the "tornado of smoke, steam and ashes." An investigation determined the boiler was weak, and as a result it called for regular inspections.

In 1898, a trainload of Stellarton miners enroute to work in Westville hit an excursion train head-on, killing both crews. Just a year later, when driver Robert Ferguson leaned out to look under the tender as his train was approaching East River Bridge, he fractured his skull on a corner of the bridge.

In 1901, a train catapulted over an embankment in a landslide near Merigomish. A brakeman named Prevost had dreamed of a white horse and convinced himself he'd seen a forerunner. He stayed in the rear of the train; his car, the first car not to go over, was left swaying in the storm over the edge of the cliff.

The Flaherty brothers opened the Egerton Tramway in 1904, with offices, car barns and a steam electricity plant at Stellarton. More than nine miles of track joined the four towns between Trenton and Westville, including a line added later to pass near the brickworks at Parkdale. Renamed the Pictou County Electric Company Ltd., they also provided electric lighting as well as transport by electric tramcars.

B. E. Fanjoy, a New Glasgow clothing store owner, is reputed to have owned the county's first automobile in 1906. James Cameron wrote that he drove "a one cylinder eight-horsepower Reno, fitted with oil-burning lamps. It came dissembled in a boxcar, and local mechanics who had never seen an automobile put it together."[12] Before Fanjoy, however, a Hopewell furniture maker had actually built a gasoline automobile — the first in the Maritimes. John MacArthur's "Victorian" two-cylinder car was completed in 1900, but its belt-drive proved deficient. After replacing this with a handmade chain and sprocket system, the auto achieved speeds of up to five miles per hour.

The horseless carriage created much consternation. Before long there were enough cars to be considered a nuisance. The Motor Vehicle Act legislated maximum speed on country roads at fifteen miles per hour, and half that in towns. Car use was permitted on Monday and Friday only. Even this was too much for the Pictou County Farmers' Association which, in 1911, petitioned the Legislature against these "devil machines," claiming the noisy machines were a menace to horses and rural folks travelling peacefully in their wagons. Later, county mayors enacted laws allowing cars on the roads on Monday,

Locomotive engineers at Stellarton, from left: J.C. MacKay, George Brown, Alec M. Fraser, W.J. Sangster, Roy Stewart, Angus Chisholm, M.D. Falconer, R.D. MacDonald, R.W. Fields, R. Somers, E. Mann, S. Skinner.

Bridge across the East River, New Glasgow

Wednesday and Friday. Their attempt to hold back progress was in vain, however, as car dealerships opened, and by 1915 at least twenty-three autos had been sold in the county. The next year the first tourists visited by car: Mr. and Mrs. James Clarke of Seattle and daughter were motoring across the continent. Mrs. Clarke was formerly Miss Forbes of New Glasgow, daughter of a Captain Forbes and niece of Mrs. Forrest MacKay.

In 1917, a man walking his horse in Abercrombie complained of a car hogging the whole road. The driver yelled to him, "Get off the road or I'll rip you up the back." The farmer described the car as having a pink stripe running around the body. "Many cars come too close, too fast, terrorize you… but this was

Booby Duff with his Maxwell, the first car in Stellarton. The first women to drive cars in Stellarton were Lib Hayes and Clara Arthrell.

the first verbal threat," claimed the *Eastern Chronicle* on July 31. The same issue discussed court proceedings in which, "failure to have car lights burning and running without a permit" earned the driver a fine of $5, while exceeding the speed limit carried a penalty of $20.

Another newly motorized vehicle generated less antagonism, according to the *Eastern Chronicle* of May 23, 1911. "Motor boat enthusiasts are elated with the movements of Mr. Cantley's new importation from England. It…outclasses anything heretofore seen on the river,…called the *Watemba*,…built for Lord Howard de Walden,…designed for racing and cruising and has a roomy cabin."

The wreck of the barque Melmerby *off Roy's Island during a violent gale in 1890 drew attention to the beautiful sand beach here, and gave the three-mile sweep of sand its name, Melmerby Beach. Pictonians rescued several crew by forming a human chain to bring the drowning men ashore.*

Thriving towns 1867-1918

By 1881 the county's population had grown to 35,535, of whom the great majority were of Scottish descent. As other nationalities moved to the area over the next thirty years, the Scots made up about 70 percent of the population. Ongoing immigration influenced the growth of urban centres. Citizens worked together to build their communities and the institutions necessary for their stability. Pictou County was as modern and self-assured a community as anywhere in Canada by 1918.

John MacKay, the elderly prothonotary at New Glasgow, ruminated on the state of settlement in 1881, "The whole face of the country is changed. In place of four log churches there are now over forty; each of which will accommodate from 500 to 900 sitters....The old canoes are replaced by a steamer which runs twice a day between New Glasgow and Pictou. In place of the mails coming monthly in a bag on a man's back, we have our mail delivered twice a day from Halifax. The travelling which took three days between the two places is now performed in four or five hours; and the saddle of Donald MacLennan is succeeded by hundreds of four-wheeled carriages, each of which may cost from £20 to £60. The price of one would buy a good farm in those days.

"The state of society, both in its moral and religious aspects, has undergone as marvellous a change as that of the physical features....The first inhabitants have passed away, and with them has also passed much of the sterling honesty,

Clarriet Morris,
New Glasgow 1912

A 1775 census listed 865 Mi'kmaqs in Pictou County; a century later, only 125 remained. Although some died of diseases like smallpox, measles, VD and tuberculosis, many starved when their preserves and food resources were usurped. When they were destitute for clothing, an uncaring government sent a few coats and blankets for the "aged and poor." Crops failed, and around 1855 "the Micmac of New Glasgow 'were ready to drop from hunger,' while in...nearby Pictou, the Indians were actually starving and crying for food."[13] They had been petitioning the governor for land since 1829, in vain.[14] After 1867, jurisdiction for aboriginals was moved to the federal government, which reserved for Pictou County's 195 Mi'kmaq people an inadequate fifty acres. Over the next sixty years, adjoining parcels which gave access to both Boat Harbour and the Northumberland Strait were acquired. In 1880, a school opened on the Pictou Landing Reserve. For survival, the men came to town to sell smelts and their crafted pick and ax handles, loops and butter tubs. Mi'kmaq women peddled mayflowers and handmade baskets and wreaths. Men found seasonal work at the Pictou Landing docks, but income from employment was erratic. Support from the Department of Indian Affairs provided a borderline existence; without fish, game and berries, many would have starved.

St. Anne's Church, Indian Island.

Pictou, East, N.S.

"Prominent and esteemed" undertaker George McLaren's business was "a very delicate one [which] involved for its successful prosecution peculiarly important qualifications which but comparatively few possess. [He] assumes the whole direction of funerals, furnishing hearse, casket, coaches, and everything necessary, personally superintending all arrangements and all calls made upon him in this connection are promptly and expeditiously attended to, while his charges will be found of a most reasonable nature." [16]

simple straightforwardness, hospitality and intense devotedness to religious matters. At one time I knew almost all the people, old and young in the County of Pictou; I am now a stranger to many of my immediate neighbourhood."[15]

MacKay's comments reflect the changing face of Pictou County as industry attracted newcomers from the British Isles, Europe and Newfoundland.

After 1880, many Blacks of Loyalist descent gave up farms in Tracadie to take work in domestic service or industry. Although not the first Blacks to live in Pictou County, scant records of others exist. In 1767, *Betsey* passenger Matthew Harris brought slaves whom Rev. James MacGregor used his mean income to free. In *That Lonesome Road*, Dr. Carrie Best writes of Black men and women slaving on a tobacco plantation at Pictou and of a slave cemetery near the Pictou-Colchester border. A mixed-race farmer called John Currie who bought land at Pictou in 1832, is buried in Haliburton Cemetery. Currie was a Virginia slave, who escaped to British territory during the Napoleonic wars, swimming out of Chesapeake Bay as bullets hit the water around him. At this time other Blacks settled near the Pictou Town Gut, but most moved on.

Pictou

Of the five towns that are the urban core of the county, the shiretown of Pictou is the oldest. Incorporated in 1873, it had gas lighting two years later. In 1887, the town was described as "one of the most thriving and enterprising towns of Nova Scotia... with elegant houses... mansions, villas, cottages, courthouse, registry office, custom house, inland revenue offices; the Pictou Bank Company have a handsome building, the YMCA a fine structure — the ground floor being utilized for the post office."[17] There were two Presbyterian churches, and one each of the Free Church of Scotland, Anglican, Methodist and Roman Catholic. Thirty-three businesses were listed, including Hamilton and Sons, who were producing half a ton a day of crackers, biscuits and confectionery. Another noteworthy business, Noonan & Davies had a reputation "as straightforward, honourable business men, and have enjoyed the fullest confidence of all with whom they have had dealings in their large business as ship brokers, commission merchants and forwading agents."[18]

A shopping tour of the downtown revealed a wide array of shops and services, including William Ross, Watchmaker & Jeweller, Engraver N. T. Mills, and Dawson, Gordon & Co. which sold London paints and wallpaper. D. Patterson featured the pure and beautifully perfumed Golden Gift Soap and choice Havana Cigars. R. D. Stiles, Druggist, "in a great measure renders the medical profession efficient....Stock is full and complete and includes a choice assortment of pure, fresh drugs and chemicals, desirable and popular patent medicines, surgical appliances, sponges, toilet articles, perfumery, fancy goods, and the usual line of druggist's sundries, as carried in all really first-class establishments."[19]

For "Gent's furnishings" D. Douglas offered suits tailored in finest worsted wool, complete with French "trouserings and fancy vest," while J. Pringle specialized in "Scotch, English, and domestic suitings, the finer worsteds, serges, yachting cloth, etc. in the latest styles...made up to order at a reasonable price and in the fashion of the day."[20] Women's dress material could be had from A. G. Baillie, Importer and Dealer in General Dry Goods, which has "ever maintained the highest of reputations for its honourable methods and sterling integrity while in the vanguard of progressive enterprise."[21]

For groceries, a shopper could make the rounds, starting with William McKeil to select tea from "the finest growths from China and Japan," or a "fragrant coffee from Java, Mocha, and South America"; then to W. S. Harris for "foreign fruits of all kinds," as well as hams, bacon, bologna and sugar-coated meats; to T. H. Pope for breakfast cereals, canned goods and "table delicacies." As well, Pope sold "a fine assortment of British and American dry goods, embracing a choice line of dress goods,...ladies' and gents' furnishings... all grades and sizes of boots and shoes... in the neatest style, sold at most reasonable prices."[22]

Mac's Oyster and Lunch Rooms were highly recommended. "The oyster is one of the most favoured delicacies of salt water products and is a strengthening and health-giving food." The restaurant, "famed for the very excellent way in which oysters in every style are served up," offered "meals...at every hour." Henderson's Restaurant was "well

known and popular [for] meals and temperance drinks," including "ices flavoured with vanilla, strawberry, raspberry, or lemon."[23]

A traveller could hire a wagon to take him from the new Pictou station to one of two hotels on Coleraine Street. The Revere boasted "over 50 bedrooms, for the most part large apartments, well-lighted and cheerful, excellent sample rooms, ladies' and gents' parlors," billiard, smoking and bath rooms. The dining room offered "choice viands and delicacies in season." The staff of fourteen paid "courteous attention" to all. Rates were $1.50 per day, with special terms for permanent boarders. Owner Mr. Rood did "quite a business in buying and selling horses, being a capital judge of horse flesh." Nearby, Central House offered "the most desirable accommodation at reasonable rates...most desirably located...near to the railway station and steamboat wharves, in the business centre of the town...with good stabling."[24]

At P. S. Brown's Billiard parlour "every convenience is at hand and the rough element is at all times excluded." The "well appointed bar" offers "choicest and purest wines, liquors and ales, tobacco and cigars.... The scientific, recreative, and fascinating pastime... of billiards may appropriately be ranked among the most popular existing at the present day, whether in public parlours or private residences." Mr. Brown, manager of the Pictou driving park, owned "Good Luck — one of the finest stallions in the province for getting trotting stock."[25]

Begun in 1893, *The Pictou Advocate* has been a major newspaper in the county for a century.

After the Fire, New Glasgow.

New Glasgow and Trenton

Upriver from Pictou, the energetic town of New Glasgow was set back when fire destroyed five acres of the business section in 1874 and several buildings the next year. Three years later the town acquired the steam pumper *Lulan* to fight future fires. The town people elected their first mayor and councillors in 1875. In 1884, the New Glasgow Electric Company built a generating plant and soon pro-

New Glasgow from the West Side

vided carbon arc street lighting. A water system was begun in 1888, and sewers were put in two years later. New Glasgow was "one of the most flourishing and picturesque towns" where "everything is as essentially Scotch as it can be after a growth of a century on the soil of America." The town boasted factories, banks, the Dominion Telegraph office, "many excellent stores, and several good hotels, two handsomely fitted up Masonic lodge rooms," churches of every denomination, and ample schools.[26]

As at Pictou, a complete range of goods and services was available. Contributing "to the pleasure, convenience, and actual necessities of the community" was J. W. Church's "very spacious and commodious" Livery Stables, which "comprise large, well-filled up stables, furnished with every modern convenience, well-lighted and drained." They accommodated up to thirty horses "of a superior and reliable stamp, kept in good condition, free from vice, sound in wind and limb and good goers." Single and double teams on reasonable terms were available for "all kinds of carriages: open and closed buggies, phaetons, surreys, dog carts, sleighs and cutters."[27]

Rev. James MacGregor had bemoaned the lack of a barber in the county when he arrived. As late as 1860, J. W. Carmichael travelled to Pictou for a haircut. No more, since popular A. McDonald's Hair Dressing Rooms opened. "A man may shave himself, certain it is that no one can satisfactorily cut his own hair. Mr. McDonald [with] long experience... cuts hair in a most artistic style, particular attention being paid to orders to wait on parties at their own homes. He has a special room for ladies, and per-

forms all dyeing operations in a thoroughly efficient manner. Razors are put in order, shears sharpened, and everything associated with a well-equipped establishment of this nature is promptly and practically executed."[28]

In New Glasgow, the commercial centre for other nearby towns, there were several insurance brokers, three newspapers among which was *The Evening News,* three national banks, the Norfolk and other hotels, numerous restaurants and recreation facilities.

In 1883, Thomas Cantley advertised thirty-four building lots, a five minutes' walk north of Nova Scotia Steel in Trenton. As workers at the steel and glass plants moved within easy reach of their jobs, churches and stores came too. King's Trenton Meat Market and A. A. Chisholm's Groceries are two shops that are still remembered.

"Strike while the iron is hot" became the motto of the town, which, when it incorporated in 1911, had a population of 1,400. The young town moved quickly to lay water mains, organize a volunteer fire brigade, dig sewers, grade roads and accredit its schools. In 1916 homes could be purchased in three new subdivisions.

Stellarton and Westville

The face of Stellarton was predominantly that of an English coal community. When Peter Barrett arrived in 1866, "it was difficult for young men to get a decent boarding house.... The sight of the old dilapidated log houses...made our hearts rebel. Such low, dirty, dingy houses, and such a herding together of the sexes, we never had seen. There were to be seen from one to three beds in the room where the cooking had to be done. I blame the General Mining Association. But they have many nice cottage rows for their employees."[29] Although Barrett's diary describes the worst of old GMA housing, the mining ghettos were never kept up like other residential areas. For example, the sewer system begun in 1903 took forty-five years to reach the Red Row mining neighbourhood. The coal companies that came after the GMA built rows of matching dwellings near the mines. Acadia Coal constructed two-storey semi-detached houses with deep yards in 1910. Among the houses standing today are ones built as temporary shelter for the influx of workers replacing miners serving in World War I. Acadia also provided lodging for single miners in the fourteen-room Black Maria and Rideout's (later Kowalski's) company boarding houses.

By 1890, 2,000 people lived in Stellarton. South and east of the mines, new residential construction was reflecting the settlement of people working on the railroad, and other related businesses. Downtown was hopping on Saturday nights — pay day at the pits. Residents could buy just about everything at the first co-operative store in the country. "It is a truism as old as the hills that 'union is strength,' and never was this more exemplified than in the case of the Union Association of Stellarton… now composed of 150 members, established in 1851. Its history since…has been one of steady progress and development…a very large and extended business as dealers in dry goods, groceries, flour, meal, molasses, boots, and shoes, hardware and general merchandise. Importing in large quantities from England, and procuring their supplies in bulk from local commercial centres, the company has every advantage, and is able to sell at prices that absolutely defy competition. The business is conducted on a solid and purely cash basis, the benefits of which are at once obvious. The quality of the goods handled is equally high, and a large comprehensive business like this has advantages not accorded smaller concerns. The premises comprise two spacious flats and a store, 26 feet x 30 feet in dimensions, with a large warehouse at the back, while employment is furnished to four hands. In all departments the stock is full and complete, the main object of the association is to keep all goods up to the highest standard of excellence, and to sell at the lowest prices consistent with a living business."[30]

In August 1866, the *Eastern Chronicle* described Westville: "Streets with clean gravelled sidewalks orna-

R. Fraser, "Druggist & Apothecary, Dealer in Drugs, Medicines, Paints, Oils, Stationery, Etc. Etc.," paid "Special attention to physician's prescriptions and family recipes, which are compounded with accuracy and dispatch by this gentleman of high professional abilities." From left: Rod Fraser, druggist P.H. McKay, Dr. J. MacDonald, Edwin Oliver, Allister Fraser.

mented with shade trees are laid off at right angles. Along these streets, neat, comfortable dwelling houses are being built, boarded and shingled on the outside and plastered inside [that] will render them comfortable in the coldest weather. There is a quiet air of neatness and cleanliness pervading the place [which] will be the most systematically laid out in the province." Soon businesses set up, including Thomas Gray's "very prominent house" for buying "British and American Staple and Fancy Dry Goods"; J. A. McDonald, who handled "only the best Groceries, Boots, & Shoes"; and George Munroe who dealt in "Staple and Fancy Dry Goods, Gents' furnishings, Millinery, Ready-made clothing, Boots, Shoes, Groceries, etc."[31]

At incorporation in 1894, the town's population was over 2,000, and there were forty-two miles of streets. During these good years for mining, Westville was a thriving centre.

Main Street, Westville

Through prosperity to war

1867–1918

Upholding the tradition established by Mortimer and Blanchard in the infant days of their settlement, Pictonians expressed a vocal and confident interest in all levels of politics. Over the years Pictou County enjoyed colourful and influential representation in both Ottawa and Halifax.

Federally the county elected two members until 1904. One of the most memorable was the first MP, J. W. Carmichael. His son-in-law, New Glasgow lawyer John H. Sinclair left this memoir about Carmichael for his family:

"A strong feeling of resentment prevailed regarding the high-handed manner in which Confederation had been brought about; many Conservatives swung to the Liberals.

The province was being cut off from the New England market and there was no prospect of anything equivalent in return. The financial terms were unfair to the people of Nova Scotia. The people were ignored and denied the right to pronounce on their destiny. Carmichael ran against Hon. James MacDonald, afterwards Chief Justice of the province. An able campaigner, MacDonald did his best to rally his forces but the tide was against him. An attempt was made to raise a religious cry against Carmichael among Roman Catholic voters."[32]

In the excitement of the election of 1869, known as the Protestant Alliance Election, Carmichael used indis-

Pictou County Council, 1895

creet language in speaking of the Roman Catholic Church. At a meeting in the Catholic stronghold of Bailey's Brook, Carmichael had barely begun to speak when a man called out asking if during the 1869 campaign he had called the Pope the Anti-Christ. "He promptly admitted he had done several foolish things in his life and this was one of them. His frank reply disarmed the Opposition, and ballots at that poll numbered 71-68 for him. He went to the first Canadian Parliament with a majority of 358."[33]

Carmichael was defeated in 1872, when two Conservatives were elected from the riding of Pictou: James MacDonald and Robert Doull. But in 1874 he and fellow Liberal, Pictou merchant John A. Dawson, won in the wake of the Pacific Railway scandal.

During Liberal Prime Minister Alexander MacKenzie's administration there was a severe depression. "Trade was dull, money scarce, prices of farm produce low. Work in towns and cities was scarce and unemployment was high."[34]

Coal trade was low, reflecting the end of Reciprocity with the United States. A protective duty was put forward, but Carmichael came out squarely and fearlessly for free trade. The miners retaliated by burning him in effigy. In 1878, the Conservatives returned to power, and the Liberals didn't elect a single member from Pictou to Parliament until 1904. Carmichael was called to the Senate in 1896 but later resigned. He died April 30, 1903.

This "striking and unique personality in a crowd looked like a chief....Big and broad shouldered with a full white beard, he had little use of his hands. To put on a collar and fasten his neckties was always more or less a test. He could not drive a nail without difficulty, nor tie a knot. He never walked for the mere pleasure of walking and was never known to run a step. He was utterly devoid of small talk and had little imagination, yet was an eager listener and an interesting companion. In his own business he was an expert....Frank open face, shaggy eyebrows over kindly blue-grey eyes that lit up and flashed when his interest was wakened... soft grey hat tipped slightly to the front and to the left side, the stick that came down heavily at each step, the brusque but kindly greeting....

"For the last years of his life his library was sort of a debating club. Night after night he sat in his old black

American Federation of Labour and T&CL Executive, New Glasgow

high-backed hair-clothed chair at the end of the table propounding his views, often very advanced on the great questions of Church and state…with his pipe well-filled and an ample supply of matches at hand and some friend who held opposite views to argue with him."[35]

His daughter Caroline reflected: "What I do appreciate, as I look back on my home life, was the conversations, particularly at the table, when we had guests, and our home was always open to visitors — hotel accommodation being poor, the Chisholm and Fraser Inns by this time were out of existence, anyone coming to town was given private hospitality.…It was at our table that I imbibed my interest in politics, for I was a listener.…The library was another rendezvous…where in an atmosphere of tobacco smoke many a political and theological discussion was carried on.…A dissertation on Free Trade was the last indulged in by the head of the house — carried on with Mr. James Ross, [undertaker]. The next morning he was over with this life."[36]

In 1882, Charles H. Tupper was parachuted into Pictou County as a Conservative candidate by his father, Sir Charles. The popular and brilliant orator who became Minister of Marine and Fisheries and of Justice served until the election of 1904. He was appreciated mainly for his vociferous support of the Pictou town rail line. Adam Carr Bell, New Glasgow druggist, former mayor and MLA, was another high-profile Conservative MP. In 1904, Liberal E. M. MacDonald was elected to what was now a single seat. In 1911, Sir Wilfred Laurier spoke at a Liberal rally in New Glasgow in support of MacDonald. On an earlier visit, the prime minister and his wife stayed with the Carmichaels. They attended Mass at Lourdes on Sunday morning and went to Westminster Church with their hosts in the evening.

Charles H. Tupper, M.P.

Another popular legislator was Duncan C. Fraser, a lawyer and former New Glasgow mayor who resigned as Government Leader of the Legislative Council to successfully contest a federal Guysborough seat in 1891.

In provincial politics, former editor of the *Colonial Standard,* Simon Holmes of Springville, was elected Conservative premier in 1878, after serving four years as Opposition Leader. His father, Senator John Holmes, had served in the legislature in the 1840s. The Liberals regained power in 1882, staying in office until 1925.

In 1886, Premier Fielding requested a repeal of the British North America (BNA) Act in favour of Maritime Union, blaming the lack of prosperity on the decline in southern markets, the development of western Canada and the dumping of central Canadian products at unfair prices. His coalition of advocates of repeal, including Pictou's Jeffrey McColl, won the election, but in the federal contest, repeal was firmly defeated overall and the issue died.

Despite a large working class, Pictonians were wedded to the traditional parties. Robert Drummond was defeated when he ran for Labour as an Independent Liberal on the Liberal slate in 1886. In his "Recollections and Reflections of a Former Trade Union Leader," Drummond recounts how he declined the offer of the seven votes of one family for the price of $15. When a committee member from his own party approached him for money to buy "hard stuff" to lubricate the voters, Drummond replied, "Not a cent, bribery is bad enough but when corruption is added it is much more reprehensible." Drummond lost the election by eleven votes. He was later appointed to the Legislative Council as a Liberal.

The next Labour candidate was P. P. Cosgrove. In 1911, the press reported he was canvassing in Westville, Trenton and Thorburn, "where he has a strong following. He is delighted with his reception in the farming districts."[37] Cosgrove lost his deposit, as did the Labour candidate in 1916.

Other than in mining, there was not a strong Labour movement in the county. For a brief time glassblowers and steelworkers had PWA lodges, but despite its all-encompassing name it remained a miners' union. Around 1890 steel workers formed a local of the Amalgamated Association of Iron and Steel Workers, an affiliate of the American Federation of Labour, but organized labour groups at Trenton and a local Trades and Labour Council during World War I did not last.

On the local level, as towns incorporated, they assumed government by elected mayor and council. Otherwise, the several villages and rural areas incorporated as the Municipality of Pictou County in 1880. Each of 24 sections sent a representative to County Council; the Council elected a warden from among its members.

The Aberdeen Hospital and nursing school in New Glasgow were opened in 1897.

Although the individual municipal governments were quick to champion their own interests above their neighbours', they were able to work together for the good of the whole county. One area where they worked together was in health reform, and the Aberdeen Hospital, opened in 1897, represented this co-operation.

Caring for the sick

Health care was gradually improving during this period. Doctors were better educated, and so better served their clientele, if Dr. Sylvanus Keith, who received patients in the Mechanics' Hall, New Glasgow, is any example. The Stellarton native advertised in 1887: "It is questionable whether there is any branch of scientific pursuit in which such wonderful progress and development have been made as in the medical profession. It is true that the philosopher's stone has not yet been found, but still the skill of the physician of the present day has done much to prolong life, and very involved indeed, must all cases be, which cannot at the present time be successfully diagnosed by him."[38]

Despite their position, doctors like Keith found themselves powerless against virulent diseases that they tried to control with yellow quarantine signs, isolating infected families from the community at large. Regular doses of sulphur and blackstrap molasses had questionable value in warding off illness, and bowls of burning sulphur proved ineffectual as diphtheria swept through family after family. Smallpox plagues struck the county several times between 1885 and 1918. Even though vaccination was available, a New Glasgow facility to confine the pestilence was bursting its walls as late as 1911. A bloody cough struck horror at the prospect of painful death by tuberculosis. Environmental concerns were non-existent: horses plied the dust or mud roads, smokestacks belched prosperity, and the waters were catchbasins for sewage and industrial waste. To combat typhoid fever, it was imperative that towns hook up to clean drinking water. Treatment for mental illness was as simple as confinement to the Pictou County Home and Asylum, which started accepting residents in 1885. At Pictou there was a marine hospital, built in 1880 and expanded in 1893, and a cottage hospital, opened in 1906. At Lourdes, Rev. William MacDonald and the Sisters of Charity opened a tuberculosis sanitorium in 1912. The Spanish 'flu epidemic, which killed over 21 million worldwide, lashed the county.

Safety and health care often walk the same path. A boy thrown from a horse, a man falling into a gravel pit, a woman electrocuted by lightning, and frequent mining mishaps were among the accidents reported in the newspapers of the time. On January 23, 1918, the Allan Mine exploded. Over several months the Rescue Corps found 88 charred and broken bodies in a mine that had been totally devastated from the blast. On March 16, in a lumber camp near West River, 21 people, including 6 children, burned to death. Many such camps were fire traps with only one door and few windows.

But tragedy and death were part of the cost of industrial development. And if there was a silver lining, it was that such disasters drew people together, helping to create a generous, compassionate community.

A New Glasgow tea party with Jessie Carmichael Sinclair, Sarah MacLeod, Seenie Howe and Anna Carmichael

Leisure and pleasure

The high energy that characterized Pictonians' industrial life between 1867 and 1918 percolated into their social life. Improved transportation and new technology offered more opportunities for recreation, at the same time, fixed working hours in industry opened up more leisure time which was spent enjoying a full range of sports and recreation. With reform promoting education, Pictonians bettered themselves through improved schooling. Throughout, they maintained their religious ties, while gradually shrugging off Victorian stuffiness to freely embrace the novelty of twentieth-century technology and entertainment.

In 1867 the values identified with Victoria's reign still prevailed. The miner, Peter Barrett, was one who personified such morals, and complained of their absence at a party he attended. "I was invited with my girl, and other young folks to attend an evening party, at a Mr. and Mrs. Smith's, Westville. It turned out to be one of those disgusting 'promiscuous kissing parties.' I felt compelled to take part for some time, until I could forbear no longer but took [my] leave, leaving my girl behind. I went to my lodgings, and then wrote a letter to the editor of the

Provincial Wesleyan, describing those kissing parties, and accordingly within a few days an editorial appeared in the above paper condemning such parties, as being 'inimical to piety and virtue.' I was at once suspected for this matter also, and soon a lawyer was employed to send threatening letters unto the editor and to me; without any result. But the young folks, and their friends, who thought that they had been insulted by the article referred to, became very angry with me. Still, I have no hesitation in saying, that these gatherings, or parties, under the 'flimsey pretext of brotherly love, sisterly love, Christian love' call it what you will, is a stepping stone to infamy."[39]

If such kissing parties were common, it seems they were mostly kept secret. People seemed to prefer getting together for more lively events. Even though manners and morals were prescribed, the Victorian Age prized enlightenment — both mystical and scientific. Indulging the rage for fortune-telling, mediums advised the trusting on the course of their lives by the way their tea leaves held the

THE EASTERN CHRONICLE

OCTOBER 9, 1890

The *Eastern Chronicle* proffered up a curious, if not amusing, collection of social tales. The following appeared in the October 9, 1890 issue:

"A meeting of the Prohibition party to select candidates for the next Dominion election chose Samuel Archibald, West River, and W. D. Taunton, editor of the *Vindicator,* New Glasgow."

"A woman belonging to the Garden of Eden attempted to take her life by cutting her throat with a razor last week. She was not in her right mind at the time."

"A country yahoo filled with No. 1 bugjuice created some excitement on Monday last walking down Provost Street. So full was he of excitement and good feeling that at times he would be obliged to stand on his toes and yell."

"The *Standard* says that Hon. Mr. Mills spoke to a crowded house on Monday night at Pictou. With the exceptions that Mr. Mills was sick at his home in Chicago and the inclement weather allowed only a small audience, the item is correct."

"At one time the electric light was our much desired benefit, but if things are not operated more satisfactorily than they have been recently, it will be one of our nuisances. Several evenings now the lights have gone out, leaving our stores and streets in darkness. Surely this can be remedied."

"As will be seen by advertising in another column, classes in painting, piano and violin culture are to be opened in this county. The teachers of this department are well known and enjoy a high reputation in their general spheres. Miss McDonald left last week for the New England Conservatory to take four weeks' study in special branches, while her past work here speaks for itself. Miss McKenzie also left last week to receive some additional ideas in her department. In Miss McKinley's violin course, special attention is given to bowing and forming purity of tone."

"A young lad named Charlie Hill, aged 12 years, and son of Mr. John Hill of this town, met with a sad accident here last Saturday evening about 5 o'clock. While attempting to board the Trenton train, he missed his footing and was crushed beneath the wheels. One of his legs was completely severed at the knee, the other foot was badly mangled and his head badly cut. He lingered a short time in excruciating agony and died about 12 o'clock the same evening. The sudden death cast a gloom over the community for some time. The boy had been frequently warned not to be going on the trains, for he had been in the habit of so doing, and it is but right that we should here still stronger warn the young boys, who now have this habit of boarding trains while in motion, to stop it as it will end in something serious as the above."

"The Gospel Temperance Society in the Methodist Church, last Sabbath afternoon was largely attended. Mr. John R. Nichols, the 'little giant of temperance oratory,' spoke for nearly an hour on the subject of Prohibition, in such a clear, practical and forcible way that could not fail to convince, if not, to convert every one of a diferent opinion. Every one present seemed delighted with Mr. Nichols' address. Another opportunity to hear this eloquent speaker will be afforded to the people of this town next Tuesday evening, in the YMCA hall. Do not fail to attend."

"On Friday and Saturday last the Boston Dramatic Co. performed in McNeil's Hall. The first night 'Rip Van Winkle' was placed on the boards and very successfully gone through with. Mr. Burrill made a capital Rip and is beyond doubt the ablest actor of the company. 'Ten nights in a Bar Room' was not so well received, nor so well gone through with, several important scenes being omitted. There were good houses on both nights."

THE EASTERN CHRONICLE

OCTOBER 23, 1890

Another issue dated October 23, 1890, had these tidbits for its readers:

"On Tuesday evening Mr. Nicholls gave one of the best entertainments in the YMCA hall that has been given here for some time. It consisted of a series of excellent views of London and its most interesting sights, which were explained in such a taking and instructing manner that delighted the audience. The instrument was one of the very best stereopticaus made and the views and lecture prepared especially for Mr. Nicholls. Unfortunately the interest attendant upon the arrival of Lord Stanley prevented a large audience, but those who were present thoroughly appreciated the very fine show given and only wish Mr. Nicholls would repeat his entertainment."

"Social circles in Montreal were shocked last week when it was known that a most popular and polished clergyman in Montreal has been leading a double life, and that at last his disgrace has come. Reverend A. B. Cruchet last summer appeared in a French Canadian village and introduced himself as Mr. Benjamin. He was accompanied by a girl of 20 years. He left the woman behind and the other day a child was born. Cruchet has confessed his wrong and will accept his punishment of guilt by expulsion from the Presbyterian Church. Many of our readers will remember the Reverend gentleman above referred to, he having laboured for some time in Pictou. About 14 years ago, the French settlement of miners who were brought to Thorburn and Stellarton, were ministered to by Rev. Mr. [sic] Cruchet."

"The dredge Canada has been at Pictou being repaired, and returns this week to Cheticamp, Cape Breton. It was expected that this dredge would, by this time, be at work on the East River dredging; but Tory promises cannot be relied on."

"A Chatham paper reports that there was a young man in that town the other day, who measured 6 f 10 in, and which beats the Pictou County man who stands 6 f, 7 in."

"Westville will have an Orange parade, social and ball, while New Glasgow, Thorburn and other places will hold socials on November 5, Guy Fawkes Day."

"Capt. Murdock McEwan of Pictou purchased the schooner Harriet, 27 tons, a few weeks ago. Unfortunately she was wrecked in the gales Sunday last near Pugwash. A total loss, no insurance."

"The ladies of the Women's Christian Temperance Union decided at their meeting on Tuesday to inaugurate for the season 'Free Saturday Night Socials' in their Coffee Rooms. The first will be held this week. A special committee of four will have charge, and promise a pleasant evening's enjoyment to young men and others who may attend."

The Itzit Theatre Band, 1914

cup or how the stars were aligned. A famous soothsayer was Mother Coo, a Christian woman whose warnings of the Drummond and Foord Pit disasters tragically went unheeded. Learned lecturers gave speeches on a variety of subjects from "Phrenology" to "The Camp Fires of Napoleon." In an 1891 lecture series Judge Fogo expounded on "Societies and Institutions," and missionary Katherine Fraser explained Armenia. Young men of the Merigomish Parliament debated such political issues as annexation to the US.[40]

Choral groups, the Westville Cornet Band, the Trenton Pipe Band and the Pictou Militia Brass Band gave concerts in halls and bandstands. To promote quality music, the Musical Association formed in New Glasgow in 1881 offered private lessons in voice and instruments. Evenings that combined music and recitation were popular, as described in the *Eastern Chronicle* of February 11, 1897: "The very best concert given in the... twin towns of Eureka and Ferrona... in Muir's Hall — that remarkable building, with 250 people... showed painful symptons of congestion. Rev. James Carruthers' readings

Trenton Theatre

of the Hibernian variety were duly appreciated. The Hon. D. C. Fraser, booked for a Gaelic reading, was very conspicuous, not so much on account of his huge bulk, as by reason of his absence." Music was provided by the James Church Quartette and the YMCA Quartette. "Miss Olding sang 'One Sweetly Solemn Thought' admirably," while Miss Eva M. Grant's "Bells of Springville" was "finely rendered."

Touring circuses, theatricals and musicians regularly visited the county. James Cameron described the first theatre built in the late 1870s in MacNeil's Hall: "The stage was complete with oil lamp floodlights, later flickering Edison electric lights, full width and height curtain, which concealed the artists in the wings and the narrow staircases which led up to dressing rooms and prop storage in the attic."[41]

For fun and for money, schools and dramatic groups staged theatricals which showcased many talented families. The MacDonald brothers of Westville played horns and woodwinds, while their sister Jeannie Hawboldt sang and acted. Stellarton's Mary Murray played the violin and directed

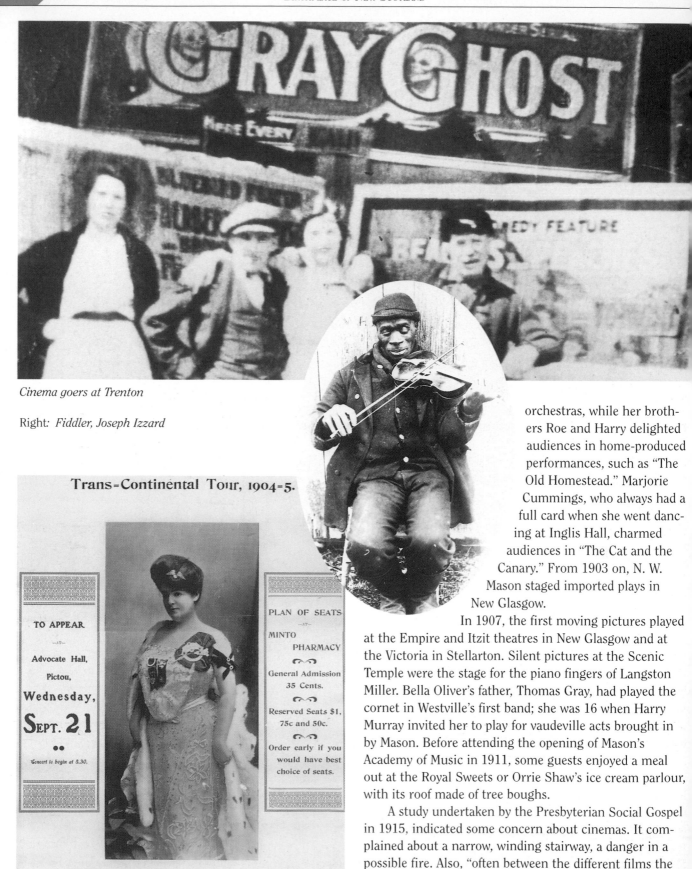

Cinema goers at Trenton

Right: *Fiddler, Joseph Izzard*

Trans-Continental Tour, 1904-5.

TO APPEAR

—AT—

Advocate Hall,

Pictou,

Wednesday,

SEPT. 21

••

Concert to begin at 8.30.

PLAN OF SEATS

—AT—

MINTO

PHARMACY

General Admission
35 Cents.

Reserved Seats $1,
75c and 50c.

Order early if you
would have best
choice of seats.

MISS JESSIE MACLACHLAN,

THE SCOTTISH PRIMA DONNA.

orchestras, while her brothers Roe and Harry delighted audiences in home-produced performances, such as "The Old Homestead." Marjorie Cummings, who always had a full card when she went dancing at Inglis Hall, charmed audiences in "The Cat and the Canary." From 1903 on, N. W. Mason staged imported plays in New Glasgow.

In 1907, the first moving pictures played at the Empire and Itzit theatres in New Glasgow and at the Victoria in Stellarton. Silent pictures at the Scenic Temple were the stage for the piano fingers of Langston Miller. Bella Oliver's father, Thomas Gray, had played the cornet in Westville's first band; she was 16 when Harry Murray invited her to play for vaudeville acts brought in by Mason. Before attending the opening of Mason's Academy of Music in 1911, some guests enjoyed a meal out at the Royal Sweets or Orrie Shaw's ice cream parlour, with its roof made of tree boughs.

A study undertaken by the Presbyterian Social Gospel in 1915, indicated some concern about cinemas. It complained about a narrow, winding stairway, a danger in a possible fire. Also, "often between the different films the jokes were low and vulgar....[The] worst feature was the number of unaccompanied children there during both

The musical Mary Murray on her wedding to Dr. R. M. Benvie,, and her brother Harry in theatrical costume.

Belles and Beaux at River John. Front, from left: *[unknown], Vida Stramberg, Louise Kitchen, Roy MacKenzie.* Back: *Emma MacConnell, [unknown], Mabel MacConnell, [unknown]*

afternoon and evening performances."[42] Many children used to hang around in front of the theatres trying to entice a someone to pay their ticket. Overall, most clergy condoned the recreation of sports, theatres, dancing, circus and singing, but considered card games sinful. Even so, 45s, crib and bridge have always been popular, and card parties were one way of raising money for a family bereaved or down on their luck.

In 1916, Standard Shows brought its "Motor Drome, Water Circus, Side Show, Museum, Mechanical City, Beautiful Orient, and a $10,000 Carry Us All" — all lit with electricity. As well as "sensational free vaudeville," Miss May Eccleston of England performed a high dive from a height of eighty feet into a tank of water only four feet deep.[43]

Outings by train to Abercrombie and Pictou Landing, or a ride in a wagon to Little Harbour were popular leisure activities for townsfolk. Cottages at Melmerby Beach and an amusement park at Bear Brook were also places to enjoy a day away from work.

In August 1900, the Pictou County Farmer's Association organized thirteen train cars of farm families for a tour and picnic at the experimental farm in Nappan. The staff of Hamilton & Sons caught the SS *May Queen* from the South Market wharf to Abercrombie where they enjoyed boat races, tug-of-war, games, and a picnic, with swinging and dancing to the Pictou Band in the evening. In the summer of 1916, the *Edith Cavell* was offering an excursion and picnic from New Glasgow to the lobster hatchery,

at 50 cents apiece. Lodge picnics were eagerly awaited, particularly in Stellarton and Westville where the July 12 Orange picnics brought trainloads from fellow lodges across the Maritimes for a grand parade followed by carnival games, dancing and a sit-down dinner in a marquee tent. Popular dances in the Bailey's Brook area at the turn of the century were "Wild 8s" and "Scotch 4s." Quadrilles were usually danced at box socials; courting was by horse and buggy.

As links to Britain were strong, the Marquis of Lorne enjoyed an 18-gun salute on a visit in 1874. When Governor Generals Lord Stanley and the Duke of Connaught visited, crowds welcomed them. Queen Victoria, though in absentia, was extravagantly feted at her Diamond Jubilee.

On June 25, 1897, the *Pictou Advocate* described a "monster picnic" in Westville hosted by Scotia Lodge of the International Order of Foresters (IOOF). Excursion trains brought crowds of sightseers, including 800 school children. The procession from the station of over 2,000 lodge members and 78th Highlanders was accompanied by the Westville, Stellarton, Sons of England and Salvation Army bands. Dignitaries extolled the glories of Britain and Queen Victoria's reign. When the queen died

Smitten by the new music technology, M.M. Haddon posed with his gramophone for his Christmas cards.

The Adam Wilson family, 1911

This solemn couple are believed to be relatives of a Mrs. A.C. Williams.

Mrs. Coll, wife of Acadia Coal General Manager Charles Coll, reads to their children. The family lived at Birch Hill, Stellarton 1900-1912.

on January 22, 1901, after reigning almost 64 years, the county wept.

The *Eastern Chronicle* reported the mourning period would last a full season. "Her death particularly affects clothiers, dealers in furnishings, and all goods connected with amusements, festivities, theatricals, and dinners. Black is the only colour displayed in shop windows throughout the Empire,...black bonnets, black clothes, gloves, neckties and hats. Dealers in black goods will be able to sell their entire stocks at a great profit. In fact, a famine in black goods threatens the English markets.

"When she started, Canada was in the midst of political upheaval and armed insurrections; now [we are] a cemented country from sea to sea."[44]

Memorial services were held in local churches; a khaki program decorated with red — to denote her military funeral — and the imperial colour purple, sold for

5 cents, the proceeds going toward the Aberdeen Hospital.

Fittingly, the week she died Reverend McLeod of Westville was lecturing the New Glasgow Literary and Historical Society on the Victorian poet Robert Browning.

Women's work

At the time of Victoria's death, new technology was entering everyday life in many ways, but especially through electricity. Plants were generating electricity for street lighting and "broomstick trains." In 1909, after transmission consolidated in the Pictou County Electric Company, power came gradually to businesses and better-off homes. Not everyone wanted it. As one man put it: "Who wants all that fire running around in the walls?"[45] Nevertheless, the considerably-brighter 25-watt light bulbs dangling from the ceiling eliminated women's daily drudgery of washing,

The Academy, Pictou, N.S.

Classmates at Pictou Academy, 1886, from left, front: *Ella Huggin; Mary McKenzie; Isabel Sproull.* Back: *Kate Murray; Jessie MacIntosh*

filling and trimming oil lamps, and the toil of scrubbing kerosene-smoked walls and curtains. After the Pictou County Power Board organized in 1921, the municipal utility strived to bring electricity into all urban homes.

The county's first telephone link was between Acadia Coal's mines and Pictou Landing piers. Public phone service began at Pictou in 1882. Telephone operators were among the first female clerical workers. Maritime Telephone and Telegraph newsletters describe the telephone operator "as invariably cheerful, polite, and

accommodating, [who] quickly smooths the ruffled feathers of a most testy subscriber. 'A low voice,' saith Wisdom, 'is an excellent thing in a woman. Let her, in short, be just, as well as courteous.'"

Anna Fraser is named as the first operator at New Glasgow, where she handled fifteen subscribers in 1888. Operator Mary Campbell recalled that when she started in 1913, they worked under "severity and strictness."[46]

Office work had been a male preserve, but the new disciplines of stenography and typing were touted as suited to women with their "aptitude for minutia and repetition." Both working class and "genteel" young women of insufficient family means saw an occupation more glamorous and better-paying than domestic service

Laura Ross, 1901

Pine Tree residents, family of either A.B. Grey or John McQueen, 1898

and shopkeeping. Even before 1900, private girls' schools in the province offered shorthand and typing. Acadia College hoped that Victorian Age girls "who might have to support themselves...will avail themselves of the excellent opportunities...for preparation in a line of work that is daily becoming more popular for young ladies."[47] A branch of Halifax's Maritime Business Academy opened in New Glasgow. Women enthusiastically embraced office work as it represented freedom. Nevertheless, once married, young women gave up their independence for hearth and family.

Although well-off women were more apt to have household help, either for a few hours a week or live-in, working- class wives and rural women worked long hours over many arduous tasks. Laundry alone was two days' work: hauling water, boiling it on the stove, scrubbing clothes on a board, preparing vats of blueing water, rinsing and hand wringing. Imagine the extra work for miners' pit

clothes! In winter she would have to shovel a path along the line, before pinning up the heavy wet garments. Clothes still damp when taken in were hung by the kitchen stove. The next day she heated heavy irons on the stovetop, then pushed them back and forth across the laundry. She did all this, as well as scrubbing, cooking, baking, sewing, sweeping, at the same time as tending to several children. Today's crafts of quilting and mat hooking were essential work at one time. Also, many working class families augmented their income by keeping boarders.

School and church

In 1880, popular subscription raised $20,000 for a new Pictou Academy containing four classrooms, a chemistry lab and a convocation hall. According to MacPhie in *Pictonians at Home and Abroad,* the school maintained its excellent reputation. Between 1880 and 1891, "a great boon was given to the Academy by the Munro Exhibitions and Bursaries offered for students matriculating into the University of Dalhousie. Five Exhibitions of the value of $400 each and 10 bursaries of $300 were presented by a former Academy student, George Munro, of New York. Academy students usually won the lion's share of these."[48]

In 1895, the school burned down when struck by lightning. A new building twice the size replaced it. By 1915, all

First United Church, Trenton archival photo of choir: Front, from left: *Eva Humphreys, Lena Crooks, Nettie Cameron, Della MacKinnon, Bessie Russel Robertson, Ellen Humphreys Aikens, Marjorie MacIssac.* 2nd Row: *Mrs. Jack MacDonald, Mary Sutherland Wadden, Mrs. Dan J. MacDonald, Ephi Humphreys, Reta Fraser Logan, Nellie Sutherland Fraser, Mary Leadbetter Coldwell, Anne MacDonald.* 3rd Row: *Hattie Powell Aikens, Eva MacDonald, Corrine Matheson Balcom, Nellie Culten MacNeil, Mrs. Blair Fraser, Margaret CatherIne MacKay, Bessie Ross Cameron, Mrs. Alfred Pace.* Back row: *Patricia Humphreys Roddam, Mrs. Ella (J.J.) Murray, Mary Logan, Lena Matheson, Margaret MacLeod, Mrs. Alf Stewart.*

of the towns had brick central schools, while in rural areas children of varying ages learned together in one- and two-room wooden schoolhouses. William Murray of Barney's River reported that as a boy he had to go in very early to light the fires, gathering his own kindling first.

As only New Glasgow and Pictou offered Grade 12, seniors from out-of-town had to get up very early to catch the train to school, and country youth often faced a long walk to the station first. Most Roman Catholics chose separate education at either St. John's Academy, or Stella Maris School, or with the Sisters of Charity at Lourdes. In 1907, Nova Scotia established a comprehensive system of technical education through evening classes in industrial

towns, such as New Glasgow. The $3 student fee was returned at session's end for good attendance. Both women and men availed themselves of this training without having to give up daytime work.

A survey in 1915 found 30 clergymen representing 43 different preaching places in the county. Church and Sunday school attendance was good in both town and country, and ladies' societies and youth groups were active. One complaint of parishioners, though, was the lack of adequate stabling provided at churches. Of 36,000 residents, two-thirds were Presbyterians united, in 1875, into the Presbyterian Church in Canada, although 38 years passed before all Church of Scotland parishes joined,

Parishoners of 2nd Baptist Church, Front row, from left: *Jean MacLean, Dolly Smithers, Rev. Constantine Perry, Ida Smithers, Rosie Paris.* 2nd Row: *Mary Bowden, James Skinner, Annie Jewell, Sadie Paris, John Clark, Esther Bowden.* 3rd Row: *Mrs. Smithers, Sam Prevae, Edward Paris, Warren Smithers, Arthur Smithers, Henrietta Jordan.*

the last being the original Kirk congregation at McLellan's Mountain. By 1911, the fifteen miles along the East River from Churchville to Kerrowgare had given 35 clergymen to the Presbyterian Church.

Meanwhile, Roman Catholic, Anglican, Methodist and Baptist populations were also growing. Heritage St. Anne's Church was erected by the Mi'kmaq population at Indian Island. The Salvation Army, which came to New Glasgow in 1885, proved popular with people of all religions for their fellowship groups and their evangelical music. In 1903, Second Baptist Church started with seven charter

Black families and pastor Rev. W. A. White, father of Portia White, a famous contralto. Second Baptist would become noted for many vocalists as the church proved to be the spiritual and social heart of the Black community.

Over this period, several Presbyterian women served in missions. Among them were Stellarton native Maud Rogers who served in Korea, Mary S. Herdman and Waterside sisters Jemima and Mary MacKenzie (both Dalhousie Medical School graduates) in India; Millsville's Annie Young in China; and teacher Bessie McCunn of River John in Trinidad.

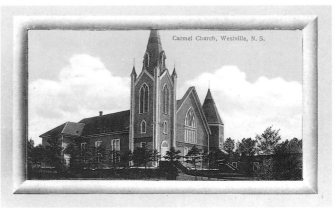

First Presbyterian Church, Pictou

Baptist Church, New Glasgow, N.S.

At home, the Presbyterian Church saw Prohibition as a vital mission, believing as the *Stellarton Star* wrote in 1909, that blind pigs and bootleggers' evil caused "fightings, clamours, tears, poverty, broken hearts, disease and death. They cause our wives, mothers, and children to hear blasphemies, curses, and foul language....Their traffic debases the mind, ruins the body and imperils the soul of all who enter their place of business."[49]

In 1904, Rev. H. R. Grant resigned his ministry to be a full-time temperance organizer, first in the county and later for the province. Col. J. J. Hickman, one of many travelling speakers, regularly preached the gospel of absti-

nence in church halls, was described in the following manner: "Whenever they stop to listen his triumph is assured, for his burning eloquence, deep earnestness, and impassioned zeal become absolutely irresistible, and he has... enrolled hundreds... after a single discourse."[50]

Sports

Pictonians liked their sports, particularly an exhilarating skate all the way from Stellarton to Pictou on the East River. Horse races on the river ice and at Cape Jack brought cheering crowds. Gradually rinks were built for hockey and curling clubs, two activities in which competi-

New Glasgow Girls' Hockey Team, 1900

SKATING ON EAST RIVER, NEW GLASGOW. N.S.

tion between the towns was hot. "Hockey Jack" Campbell who played for Westville is said to have been the first in Nova Scotia to use the wrist shot. At New Glasgow's Union Track in 1911, racing was a live issue.

Cricket continued popular with two provincial championships coming to Stellarton between 1905 and 1910. In 1896, a county quoit association was formed. Trenton and the mining neighbourhoods vied for the assocation trophy; Victor Fleury of Westville is said to have written the quoit rulebook. The popular spectator sport of baseball allowed athletes like Harry Saunders and the Ferguson brothers to shine. The Pictou County baseball league folded into a provincial league in 1911.

The YMCA introduced basketball to the county. In the early 1890s, Stellarton's Rev. Finlay MacDonald and New Glasgow's John G. Thompson played at the Y College in Springfield, Massachusetts, on the founding team. YMCAs

New Glasgow Football Team, 1890. Back row: *D.A. McKinnon (Umpire), Joe. F. Fraser, D.K. Grant, David Fraser, John Fraser, D. Campbell.* Middle row: *F.H. Coops, James Fraser, Williard Thompson, George Patterson, captain, Henry Graham, Neil Matheson, Rod. McColl.* Front row: *A.D. McRae., E. McLeod, E. McKay.*

Tennis Courts, Stellarton, N. S.

were considered a healthy venue for youthful sports. In 1891 a series of fundraisers for a Y building by five New Glasgow ladies included an excursion to Egerton, a promenade concert and a garden party. Already the Boy's Branch was making good progress at dumb-bell drill twice a week. A golf club that became the Abercrombie Golf Club formed in 1907.

In 1915, New Glasgow had a supervised playground with swings, tilts, volleyball, baseball and sandboxes, open six weeks in the summer. The New Glasgow tennis club had 192 members, while Stellarton's had 70. Both men and women enjoyed this sport not only in town, but also on the village courts at Springville and McLellan's Brook. The most popular games played at schoolyards were baseball, blind man's bluff, dodge, hide 'n seek, fox and goose, king in the yard and puss in the corner.

The Great War, 1914-1918

Social activities moved backstage in 1914, after the British Empire went to war with Germany — a blood bath beyond any experience. This was not the first time Pictonians had risked their lives in battle. Before settling here, many had served in British wars, including the Boer War. Many from the Pictou Militia were the first to sign up for World War I. As well as serving in the ground forces, Pictonians joined the navy and the fledgling air force. Even the 78th Militia Regiment Band enlisted, becoming the regimental band of the 85th Overseas Battalion, Nova Scotia Highlanders. The talented musicians provided welcome relief from the grim, gruelling fighting. Among medical personnel who served, three nurses from Pictou County were with the first Canadian troops to go to France. *The Pictou Advocate* of December 18, 1915, features Myrtle Granton of Pictou, who was in charge of the operating room of No. 2 Canadian Stationary Hospital, at Latouquet, France. Major Margaret Clothilde MacDonald, who nursed in the Boer War, was matron-in-chief of the Canadian Army Nursing Service in World War I.[51]

Canada's first and only battalion of Black soldiers was Pictou County based. When Canadian Blacks came forward to fight

Hopton family soldiers, from left: *son, Sidney; father, James; son, William.*

for their country they discovered they were unwelcome to serve alongside of Whites. After an outcry, they were invited to join the No. 2 Construction Battalion, head-quartered at Market Wharf in Pictou. They later transferred to Truro. Several Blacks from New Glasgow were among the 300 Nova Scotians in the battalion. In March 1917, aboard the SS *Southland,* they sailed over-seas through submarine infested waters and eventually supplied timber to the front lines in the Jara mountain region in France. Their hospital and recreation facilities were segregated, and although they were not permitted to fight at the front, some indeed did, and eighteen of the battalion died there.

An eighteen-year-old tuba player and bugler, John G. MacDonald of Westville, was the first Pictonian to die in this war, in January 1915, of pneumonia. During the war years, the dreaded letters and telegrams announcing the death of a soldier were all too frequent. Almost every issue of a paper carried the news that a fighting man had fallen, and offered condolences to the family. On one occasion the provincial film censor was called to task over "grossly crude fake fighting scenes" in *Called To the Front* — a docudrama playing in local cinemas. "Such sensationalism should not be permitted because of the heartbreak people are already enduring."[52]

By the time the armistice of November 11, 1918, was signed, more than 400 Pictou men and women had given their lives in the Great War, while many returned home with permanent injuries. Sobered by its tragic experience in international conflicts, Canada had truly come of age.

CHAPTER 4

Kindling the embers of industry

1919–1945

It is an indisputable fact that the end of World War I coincided with the beginning of deindustrialization of the Maritimes, the cause of which has been widely debated by scholars for many years. In Pictou County, as elsewhere, both mining and steelworking declined, never to regain their former glory, and as the backbone industries weakened, so did many smaller manufacturers. Survival favoured those with diversified markets, and those who modernized tools and products. Although by 1927 steel and coal were experiencing some growth, the Great Depression undermined this recovery. As productivity declined in all sectors, pay envelopes became fewer and thinner, so the downturn was also felt by retail-

ers. In food production, expansion appears to have been limited to strawberries and lobsters.

The ailing economy reflected itself in labour unrest. While the 1925 coal strike brought out the best in community spirit, the populace became resentful when, a few years later, Nova Scotia Steel and Coal (NSSC) went into receivership. As well, the county grieved through several mine explosions.

Providing some excitement in these tough times, the county welcomed its first airplane and opened an airport. From the late 1930s came a move toward home ownership for the working class. Party politics were largely opportunistic, according to newspaper reports, though individual representatives were known to

Allan Shaft miners, 1934: L-R: Front, seated: *Garfield Murphy, John Pitts.* First row: *[unknown], Howard Desmond, Harlan Stewart, James Carrigan, James Borden, Percy Myers, Alfred Bodak, John Kapatanza, John Scott, Teddy Donnelly, William Billick, Millan Grant, Archie Darroch?, William Mattie, Murdo MacLeod, Richard Clark, Alfred Hand, Charlie Morgan, Charlie Arnold, Abraham Hennessey, Dan Gammon, Anthony Murphy, Hector Marcipont?, August Marcipont, John Kalansky, James Murphy, Joseph Nicholson, Egnate Bortniak, Frank Weeks.*

The Allan Shaft

Acadia Rescue Corps: Colin Jamieson, David Cullen, Roderick Martin, Dominic Nearing, and Ted Simpson. The county mines had acquired a fearful reputation, despite being well-engineered and managed. Spontaneous combustion is deemed to have caused at least 5 of the 8 explosions over the Allan's 47 years, the worst being the heartbreaking "holocaust" in 1918, which put 88 black wreaths on doors. In the 1924 explosion, four men suffocated in carbon monoxide when they were trapped behind a coal fall. Luckily, the pit was idle when blasts in both 1929 and 1932 devastated the pit. In 1935, seven miners perished in an explosion. The community had become grimly adept at dealing with tragedy. Since 1911, a self-contained breathing apparatus had been used which allowed a corps of trained draegermen to enter mines after an explosion to save men and mines. The Acadia Rescue Corps became world-famous for their courage and their showing in international competitions. They quickly offered their services at the Moose River gold mine cave-in in 1936, where three Ontario men were trapped for 11 days. Leading the way through a precarious abandoned rock tunnel were the Acadia Rescue Corps and Drummond miners with superior skills in roof support, under the direction of their engineer C.D. Samson.

put the county first. The temperance movement, which had loomed large for a century, was finally put to rest when Prohibition was lifted. Though moving pictures and travelling spectacles were popular with those who could afford them, much entertainment was home-grown, such as church excursions, dances and parades.

When Canada entered World War II, Pictou's main industries were revitalized, and the county once again prospered, although the price was the lives of young men sent to the Front.

2nd Row: *Harold Lowe, Harry Ballantyne, Albert Williams, Russell Paris, William Borden, Joe Robertson, Tommy Connors, John MacKenzie, Robert Young, Jim MacEachern, William Haggerty, James Kennedy, Everett Hale, John Patterson, Bert Mason?, Lionel Fitt, Clarence Best, John Mishken, Bert Doyle, John MacEachern, Eddie Fleming, Harold Halliday, William Moss, James Harvey, Raymond Scott, James Izzard, John Pentz, Cecil Ward, Roddie MacNeil, Ernie Slater, George Frazer, Calvin Davidson.* Standing (back): *Alex MacLeod, James Duff, Henry Bigney, William Terris, Robert Doyle, Dennis Lawlor, Henry Cameron, Roy Davidson, Peter LeChambre.*

Coal

Looking first at mining, by 1920 coal mining had fallen to pre-war levels. The Maritime market was no longer expanding once industries consolidated in central Canada. Moreover, freight rates made Nova Scotia coal uncompetitive in Ontario, despite tariffs on imported American coal. Reflecting the times, the industry rationalized. Pictou County's own NSSC bought Acadia Coal in 1919. Two years later, the British Empire Steel Corporation (BESCO), which owned Dominion's coal and steel properties in Cape Breton and Springhill, took over NSSC. As well as being responsible for 85 percent of the province's coal output, the integrated BESCO owned iron mines, steel plants, finishing mills, coal freighters, 272 miles of railway and the Halifax shipyards. BESCO reorganized as Dominion Steel and Coal Corporation (DOSCO) in 1928.

Coal sales fell during the early 1920s, at the same time the company actively reduced costs, including wages. Finally, in 1925, after enduring a six-month strike, colliers with Acadia returned to work with a 6-8 percent wage *cut*. The industry gradually picked up, with employment remaining steady until 1930 at Acadia's mines and at Intercolonial's Drummond mine in Westville. However, coal sales fell severely during the Depression, and mine wages fell to half of 1929 levels by 1932. Meanwhile, the

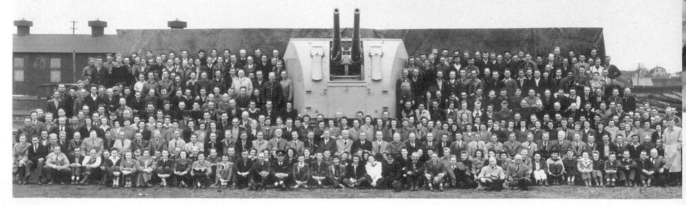

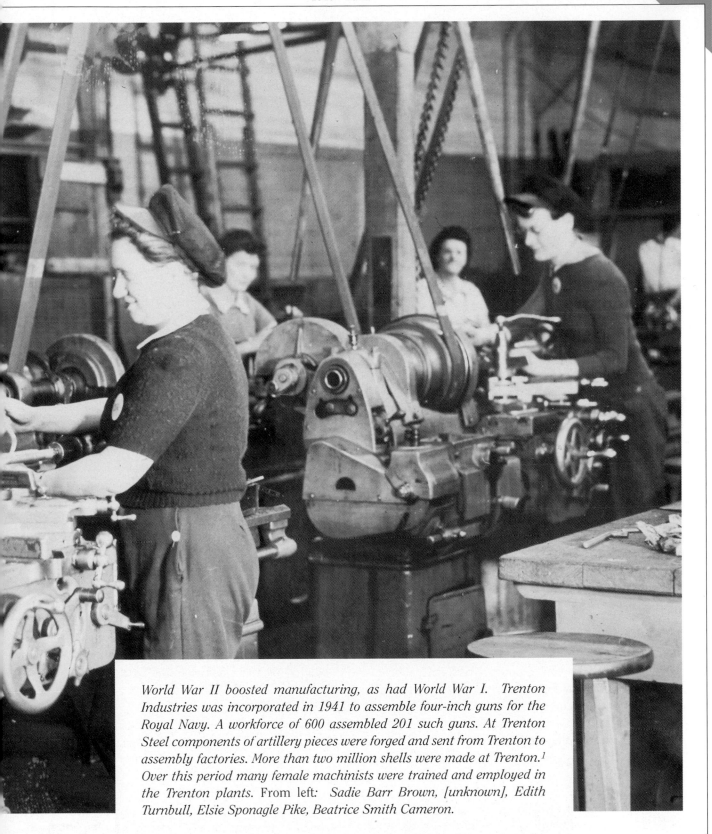

World War II boosted manufacturing, as had World War I. Trenton Industries was incorporated in 1941 to assemble four-inch guns for the Royal Navy. A workforce of 600 assembled 201 such guns. At Trenton Steel components of artillery pieces were forged and sent from Trenton to assembly factories. More than two million shells were made at Trenton.[1] Over this period many female machinists were trained and employed in the Trenton plants. From left: Sadie Barr Brown, [unknown], Edith Turnbull, Elsie Sponagle Pike, Beatrice Smith Cameron.

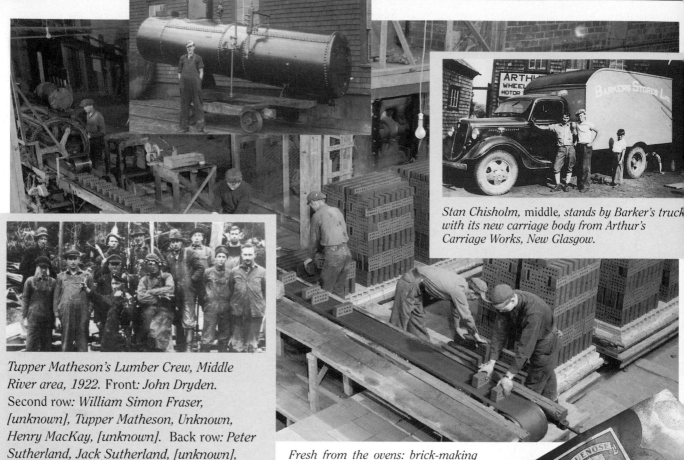

Stan Chisholm, middle, stands by Barker's truck with its new carriage body from Arthur's Carriage Works, New Glasgow.

Tupper Matheson's Lumber Crew, Middle River area, 1922. Front: *John Dryden.* Second row: *William Simon Fraser, [unknown], Tupper Matheson, Unknown, Henry MacKay, [unknown].* Back row: *Peter Sutherland, Jack Sutherland, [unknown], [unknown], [unknown].*

Fresh from the ovens: brick-making at Parkdale

Amalgamated Mine Workers (AMW) formed in opposition to the UMW. The latter, through their U.S. headquarters and flamboyant leader, John L. Lewis, were considered to favour their American members in the central Canadian market. The two unions clashed — sometimes violently. Their differences tore apart mining families that were already strained from hardship. Amid this tension, Acadia's parent NSSC went into receivership. The miners had to take a cut in their already meagre wages to help, as they put it, "buy the company out of receivership."[2]

In 1935, the coal industry started to recover, in line with the overall economy, although NSSC wasn't discharged from receivership until 1938. World War II revitalized mining. Men worked double-shifts putting out coal, while many who had left to take advantage of increased activity at the Pictou shipyards were recalled, and a freeze was put on miners enlisting.

Under BESCO, steelmaking diminished. By selling NSSC to an outside conglomerate with competing interests, any implied social contract that the previous owners might have exercised with their local employees was lost. BESCO didn't invest in modernization at Trenton, so the plant became less competitive and efficient. For workers

that meant lower and unsteady wages. BESCO closed the cogging mill at Trenton in 1921 (and the NSSC steel mill at Sydney Mines) in favour of Sydney's Dominion works. On top of this, both Trenton Steel and Eastern Car were adversely affected by the Depression and the receivership of NSSC. In the 1930s the plant was barely running. Then, in 1943, more than 500 men lost their jobs when BESCO's successor, DOSCO, closed the nut and bolt and the milling departments of Trenton Steel.

When the economy prospered, the progressive Eastern Car and Wheel Foundry manufactured train cars. Over time, a wide assortment of rail freight cars rolled out of the plant, including pit and coal cars, chemical and insulated carriers. From Pictou Landing the company shipped around the world, even as far as Argentina when Russia refused to accept its order of flatcars after World War II.

In 1937, employees of NSSC's Trenton plants finally unionized. Local 1231 of the United Steelworkers of America became affiliated with the Canadian Congress of Labour, and it represents Trenton workers to this day.

"White Boots" — a Coalburn Bull owned by the Dickie family, worked at stump pulling and ploughing

Shipbuilding

Pictou shipyards thrived during World War II, and the Pictou Foundry and Machine Company, owned by the Ferguson family since 1904, repaired 250 corvettes, minesweepers and Castle Class corvettes. Also, between 1941 and 1945, twenty-four 4,700-ton cargo vessels were built by Foundation Marine. At their busiest, the four-berth yard turned out one ship per month and employed 3,000 men and women. Many commuted from rural areas and the upper towns, while transient men lived in a staff house. Later, prefabricated housing was erected for families.

Manufacturing

Many manufacturers in Pictou lost their share of the market for two significant reasons. Firstly, freight rates greatly increased the price of shipping to central Canada, and secondly, Montreal and Toronto business interests bought local firms and then closed them down in order to minimize competition.

Other businesses, however, survived. J.J. Cumming in 1921 installed the first electric steel casting furnace in the Maritimes, and increased their capacity four-fold in 1929. Cumming became Maritime Steel and Foundries Ltd. in 1939. Diversification proved the saviour for Cameron and

Fraser, who expanded their woodworking operation into coffins. Kilns in Parkdale made bricks. Although the lumber business was hit by the drop in pit timber demand, Tupper Matheson moved his father's Middle River sawmill to Westville, and continued in business. Numerous small concerns manufactured products used locally, including Westville's Crockett Brothers who made metal creamery supplies, and Sunny Brae's Bluenose ax handles.

An intriguing representative of the bottling industry was Trenton's Greenhill Company, maker of Chuckles pop from 1929 to 1932. Other shortlived ventures include

One of the Broidy ships was the MV Amacita, which Broidy bought after it had been seized for rum-running under the guise of a lobster boat: lobsters were packed in ice on top to conceal kegs of rum underneath.

Feeding impounded lobsters

The expression "milk route" had real meaning as the train from Sunny Brae stopped frequently along the line picking up milk jugs for delivery to Picoda Dairy.

Riverbank Manufacturing that made seaweed sheet insulation until a blight destroyed the supply. A last mill at Eureka made netting for 13 years before yet another fire in 1933 finished the textile industry there. The automobile forced Hattie Brothers' manufactured wagons and sleighs off the road.

As the above sampling of activity indicates, the former industrial centre, Pictou County was in decline.

Farming and fishing

Industrialization had taken many rural folk off the land to live and work in town, so the number of working farms dropped over the first decades of the 1900s. That left farm labour in short supply, even as agricultural production remained important for the local populace. Most farmers cultivated assorted crops and raised livestock.

In rural life everything has its season. A farm wife wrote of the spring, 1919:

"May 20: Warm day, the night is cool. Barry went to town today on a pleasure trip, although his fencing and crop is so far behind. The cow calfed after dinner.

"May 22: Warm day and putting out manure, as Barry finished fencing yesterday. I done no gardening yet — it's the same old story with me. Can't do near all I likes to do.

"June 15: We are enjoying the longest days. Planted

etc. last of the potatoes Monday and put the turnips in…. Sold two loads of potatoes in Stellarton."[3]

Fall meant the harvest. In the first half of the twentieth century big threshing machines were rented out to farmers for harvesting their grains. Hay was another important crop, necessary to feed dairy cows in winter. During the 1920s and 1930s, farmers from Springville and Bridgeville organized strawberry shipments to Montreal, Boston and points in between. At least once a week farmers drove their wagons to town to sell their butter, eggs and vegetables.

Lobsters continued to be the most valuable ocean resource, even though the Great Britain market did not come back after World War I. William Broidy of River John initiated the shipment of live lobster to New England in 1927, when the first refrigerated express car left Pictou for Boston with 20,000 pounds of crustaceans. Pictou became the headquarters of Broidy's Maritime Packers whose sphere of influence expanded to include the whole of the Gulf of St. Lawrence. Other seafoods, such as herring and crab, were also processed.

Transportation

Fishermen were by now benefiting from motorized boats, just as cars had become the preferred method of transport

In winter motorists often shortened the drive to Pictou from upriver towns by driving across the ice in Pictou harbour.

The Vendome Hotel, near the CNR station, New Glasgow

on land. In 1923, Nova Scotia converted from left to right-side driving. Until roads were paved, cars were put up on blocks for the winter, in favour of sleighs and public conveyance. They remained out of commission until May 24, when the roads were deemed dry enough. Major road paving in the county was underway by the mid-1930s. In 1939, Northumberland Ferries ran the first car ferry from Caribou to Charlottetown.

In 1926 the Pictou County Power Board bought their first bus, to run from Trenton to New Glasgow. Their sec-

ond bus they built in their own barns. When finished, it was too high to pass through the doors so they had to deflate the tires, ease the bus out, then refill the tires in the open. More buses were acquired, so that by May 7, 1931, the last tram ran from New Glasgow to Stellarton, driven by Dave Thompson. Long-distance bus service came seven years later.

Airplanes were attracting much excitement, as a woman of Six Mile Brook wrote in her diary on November 14, 1919: "It's after 11 and I am near froze, but I must write. We saw the first 'airplane' pass today."[4] Over the

next few years planes visited the county, including at the *Hector* celebration in 1923. One accompanied a circus, another turned up offering the thrill of 10 minutes in the sky for $5. Serious aviation began when a flying club was organized and a runway was put in at Trenton, where the first plane landed on June 27, 1932.

The last attempt at railway building in the county was the infamous Guysborough Railway — the biggest boondoggle in the province's railway history. Before every vote, politicians touted the line which would open the Eastern Shore to inland markets, but between elections they fell

victim to amnesia. The line was discussed as early as 1897. The Pictou County portion was to run from New Glasgow through Sunny Brae to Country Harbour. Work finally began out of Sunny Brae in 1929. Sixty-seven miles of roadbed and trestles had been put in when the Canadian National Railway (CNR) stopped the work in 1931, purportedly for financial reasons. A completed section from Sunny Brae to just beyond Eden Lake—the Guysborough spur—was used for shipping lumber until 1958. Several Eastern Europeans who laboured on this line settled in Pictou County.

Daily living, good times and bad

1919–1945

Neighbourhoods

By 1921, the 40,851 people of Pictou County were living
in housing deemed generally good, except for some
older coal company dwellings. Mining ten-
ants had to rely on the company carpenter
for repairs, though they could spruce up
their homes with whitewash and flower beds.
Once Acadia Coal started selling houses to
employees in the 1930s, the faces of these neighbourhoods brightened. Company housing in Westville had
been privatized years earlier. The mostly mining families
who comprised the Stellar Group — the first co-operative housing on mainland Nova Scotia — were in their
homes by 1942. The move represented freedom from
ghetto living and the tyranny of company-owned housing. Enthusiasm for co-ops led also to other communal
ventures, such as stores, Northumberland Co-operative
Fisheries and the Alexander Beaton Credit Union.

The early 1940s brought more house construction when R. K. Delong bought a large land tract and
sold building lots in the Vale Road area. During the War
industrial activity resulted in Eastern Woodworkers pre-
fabricating housing in Pictou and the north end of New
Glasgow. All five Pictou towns boasted large elegant
houses that reflected the wealth generated by industry.
Many of the business and professional people who
resided in them also owned cottages at the shore.

Health improved. Virulent diseases such as smallpox
diminished due to vaccination and an overall improvement in sanitation. Pictou's Sutherland Harris Memorial
Hospital opened in 1928. The Aberdeen Hospital in New
Glasgow and nurses' residence expanded. After their
obstetrics wing opened in 1922 the incidence of mid-
wife-assisted home births started to decline.

Door-to-door traders brought produce directly to
households. In addition to farmers selling produce,
there were butcher deliveries. A vendor would open the
back of his horse-drawn wagon so the customer could

Thomas Cantley Mansion

select a cut; then he sliced the meat on his board and placed it on the customer's platter. Old-timers remember Frank Sobey delivering meat from his father's butcher shop in Stellarton. Today Sobeys' grocery chain is just one part of their business empire. Robert Hoegg recalls the ice cream man, George Van Loco, who went "up and down the neighbourhood streets ringing his bell. He had a wagon with a hood on it, painted white. His nice horse sported red ribbons, and a shiny brass bit. George wore a white coat and a white hat. You could get an ice cream for 5 cents. If you wanted, he would

put six scoops for 25 cents in your bowl."[5]

In March 1925, Barker's Grocers were delivering a 98-pound bag of Quaker flour for $6, a 30-pound box of boneless codfish for $3.90, their best molasses for $1 a gallon, and baked beans at 15 cents a tin. At neighbourhood stores like Alaffe's in Stellarton the customer presented her "store book" to record such purchases as kerosene, molasses and tobacco. The account was settled on pay day. Working class people bought mostly on credit and once a week paid collectors who came around. Robert Hoegg remembers a man named Diamond from Westville: "He sold a bit of furniture, oilcloth, things like that. You could go and buy from him. He'd come knocking on your door every Saturday. I remember he went to one house, and the woman sent her boy to tell him she wasn't home. He said to the kid, 'the next time your mother goes away, tell her to take her feet with

The Sutherland Harris Memorial Hospital

The Stellar Housing Co-operative on top of Claremont Avenue. Front Row, from left: Myrtle Steeves, [unknown], Dorothy Dean, Sadie MacPherson, Lucy Price. Back: Vince Mahar, John "Nip" Sample, John Dean, George MacPherson, Roz Price, Frank Buck, Elton Steeves.

Rory MacKenzie's Butcher Shop, Westville. From left: [unknown], Donald Hayman, Rory MacKenzie, [unknown], MacKenzie's son.

Ryan's Grocery, Archimedes Street, New Glasgow

her.' She was hiding behind the door and he could see her feet."[6]

In time the national chain stores, such as Woolworth's and the Metropolitan, moved in to compete with local businesses some of which advertised their wares as follows.

George Mamy's grocery shop, next to his Trenton Dry Goods Store, offered "Special bargains all this week." The London Fruit Store's Sea Foam Kisses at 29 cents a pound and their pecan and butternut rolls were "the best candy ever made in New Glasgow," while their "sanitary kitchen" served sandwiches, malted milk, hot bovril and oyster stew. Vineberg and Goodman opened "Our Exclusive Men's and Boy's Shop" in the former Itzit Theatre building. In 1926, car dealers D. R. MacKay & J. O. MacLeod were offering one Cadillac, one Reo, one Jewett, two Durants and one Dort at special prices and with an easy payment plan. Thorburn grocers McKay and Co.'s pledge to stay "with you in bad times and good," reminded miners of the merchant's support during the big strike in 1925. "Say it with Flowers," advised Stellarton's George McLaughlin, who specialized in floral designs for weddings and funerals. In Westville, R. Fraser's Rexall Store sold "The Usual Reliable Seeds" while dry goods merchant George Moussa was giving $1 free for every $10 spent.[7]

In October 1927, it was announced that Pictou colliers had produced 74,616 tons in the last year and that
the steel works had its highest payroll in three years.
Retail trade prospered accordingly, bolstered by the
growing number of American visitors in summer. Then
the 1929 stock market crash precipitated the Great
Depression. Retailers, like industry, endured losses and
closures for many years and did not recover until heavy
industry started rolling again in World War II.

Politics on the move

Pictou County's representation in both federal and
provincial governments from 1918 to 1925 mostly mir-
rored the parties in power. Thomas Cantley sat in
Parliament from 1925 until assuming a Senate seat in
1935. In the election of that year, a former Conservative
was leading a new political movement intended to over-
come the Depression. Reconstruction was vowing "a
better deal for all." The party and its local candidate, the
Rev. P. Lewis, failed to inspire. The Liberal Party took

the country. Liberal H.B. McCulloch held the county
seat until 1957. In 1940, the Co-operative Common-
wealth Federation (CCF) attempted to win seats in
Pictou County but was unsuccessful. The Communist
party made very little impact. When Tim Buck visited

MR. THOMAS CANTLEY.
First Vice-President and General Manager.

*Thomas Cantley, M.P.,
later Senator.*

the home of Amalgamated Mine Workers President Frank "Timber" Munroe in 1934, the union was damaged by infered communist influence. The CCF, under the name of Labour-Progressive, ran in the 1945 federal election and got 323 votes.

In 1920, in the first provincial election in which females could vote, Bertha Donaldson ran for Labour without success. One Labour candidate, Trenton machinist Henry Fraser, came within forty-four votes of defeating the sitting Liberal, R.M. MacGregor.[8]

The Tories reassumed provincial power in 1925. Before they were voted out of office in 1933 they abolished the appointed Legislative Council.

Prior to this election the Franchise Scandal exposed corruption in the returning officers' voters' lists. In Pictou County alone, 3,000 voters were deleted. Eventually all were registered, though many stood in line for hours, while the returning officers made the process as painful as they could.

Patronage was another issue during this campaign. A story put out by the Liberal camp told of "a highly paid female investigator" visiting a New Glasgow widow receiving Mothers' Allowance. She had 10 children, one of them disabled. When asked what her late husband's politics were, the woman "proudly answered Liberal. She never heard of Mother's Allowance from that day to this."[9]

Law and order

Politics aside, Pictou County residents have by and large been a law-abiding group, except in one area — the sale and consumption of alcohol — where the law was flouted by all walks of society. Although temperance advocates zealously persisted in their war against booze, Prohibition was a joke. Liquor was condoned by law-makers and law-enforcers. During elections, rum flowed freely to reward workers and buy votes, while police and inspectors often forewarned bootleggers of a raid. At best, the transgressor paid a token fine then returned to business. Clifford Rose, a former inspector, said he had to be a combination of "lawyer, policeman, politician, fox and lion," as well as lucky. He recalled his four years of adventure, comedy, danger and tragedy raiding "dives." After dashing in and making a grab for the evidence — washtubs of beer, jugs of rum — and trying to prevent the proprietors from pouring it down sinks, a fight would ensue, while cans of rum were flying out the windows. In 1928, Rose collected over $10,000 in fines, while legal vendors were authorized to sell liquor by prescription only.[10] A surviving legal vendor's book contains the names of several upstanding citizens who needed liquor for medicinal purposes. Finally, the provincial government decided to take their share of the profitable business when a 1929 referendum approved government liquor stores.

When people reminisce about this period they talk about safely walking outdoors at all hours, leaving doors unlocked even while sleeping, and the absence of crime in general. An esteemed and memorable lawman was Peter Owen ("Peachie") Carroll, who became Pictou's chief of police in 1884, and retired as a detective with the provincial force in 1922. Most of Peachie's career was in Pictou, although he also garnered renown in the Klondike and in British Columbia. Through a combination of cunning and pluck, this accomplished detective trapped safe-breakers, thieves, illegal distillers, burglars and murderers across the Maritimes.[11]

There were two notable hangings in this time in Pictou. The first was an Italian miner named Carrari who, in June 1917, murdered another Italian immigrant, Peter Marablito. Marablito's wife was having an affair with Carrari. The adulterers got her husband drunk and killed him with a meat cleaver. Police Chief Watters found the body in the bushes the next day. Mrs. Marablito died in jail; Carrari was hanged on January 30, 1918.

The Pictou Advocate of Sepember 2, 1921, described the hanging of a man named Loder for the murder of Daniel Barry of Pictou. The self-confessed murderer was executed at 3:05 a.m. "He walked with unfaltering steps through the jail yard and up the scaffold steps. He uttered not a word on the way.... A crowd had gathered, many scaled the high board fence in order to get near the gallows that were completely enclosed. Several auto parties from nearby towns" also came to the hanging. Loder was interred "alongside the Italian who was hanged a few years ago."

CAPTURED A FIRE BUG

Owen "Peachie" Carroll

A murder that still intrigues dates from the spring of 1930, when elderly Glengarry woodsman John Dryden was murdered with an ax while he slept. William MacDonald, a recent Irish immigrant, was arrested after pawning Dryden's watch, but he was not convicted after he described how two others were responsible. However, when he was asked to be star witness he refused to testify. MacDonald served three years in prison for contempt; the others, James Stewart and Arthur Fisher of Glengarry were not convicted. The case, still unsolved, contains a further twist of intrigue because the man that MacDonald claimed as his alibi, William Welsh, disappeared at the time of the murder. Police dragged lakes, combed the woods, searched steamship lists, and train passengers, but Welsh was never found. Around the time of Dryden's murder, a car was reportedly stopped at an abandoned water-filled mine at New Lairg. Agonizing human screams were heard. Could Welsh's corpse lie in the old copper pit?

At the Stellarton jail on MacKay Street, from left, are believed to be: Pictou Sheriff Harris; Arthur Fisher; James Stewart; and Stellarton Police Chief Sam Baker.

The foxtrot and a bucket of blueberries

New Glasgow's *Evening News* still advertises social events and entertainment as it did in the 1920s and 1930s. When moving pictures were still a novelty, Charlie Chaplin was starring in *The Vagabond* shown at Trenton in July 1920, while *A Girl at Bay* was playing at the Crescent in Westville. Tickets ranged from 50 cents to $1.50 to see *The Original Katzenjammer Kids* at the Academy of Music — "the great cartoon fun show with a multitude of pretty girls and famous chorus of 25 under 20 [is] a whirl of beauty." Late in the decade silent movies gave way to talkies. For Christmas 1929, appearing at the Roseland was *Innocents of Paris* with Maurice Chevalier, billed as "the world's great-est entertainer, straight from the gay boulevards and Folies Bergere of Paris." The Jubilee in Stellarton was offering the jungle adventure *Where East is East*.

The tents were packed at a twenty-one-event Chautauqua in the summer of 1920 that featured the Swannee River Quartet and Dr. E. B. MacDowell's lecture "Around the World." More than 600 crowded the New Glasgow arena on November 10 for the 1925 Industrial Fair, including a large contin-gent brought by special train from Thorburn. Charles Roy won the door prize—"a generous sized, high-class cured ham." Danny the Halifax Trick Dog performed stunts under the direc-tion of his owner. The Melody Boys Orchestra was a genuine delight, while the MacLeod Axe Company exhibited their "made in New Glasgow" products.[12] The following evening a Scottish pro-gram featured reel, pipe music and sword danc-ing, directed by Pipe Major William Wilson of 78th Band, one of several bands in the county.

In August 1933, the *Eastern Chronicle* reported that "the talented children of Melmerby Beach presented [their annual play] on the verandah of Dr. & Mrs. Melville Cumming." The comedy *The Lengthy Marriage* was fol-lowed by Miss Katherine MacDonald dancing the Highland Fling. The main attraction was *The Enchanted Teapot*: M. A. Archibald played the Empress; Harold Sinclair was Prince Orion; Norman Sinclair was the prime minister; Katherine Cumming was the fairy queen; Stewart MacCulloch played Hoity Toity; and Norrie Douglas played Rosabelle. The $11.35 that was raised was donated to the milk fund.

Outings to the beach or to Green Hill Lookoff and the Pioneer Museum were popular. The parade and boat races at the annual Lobster Carnival attracted many people to Pictou, including Babe Ruth. At the Gyro Ball in 1927, the *Evening News* reported that over 300 "had the time of their sweet young lives." The "most gracious chaperones" were Mrs. Dr. V. T. Parker, Mrs. James Milne and Mrs Oswald MacLeod. The event featured 23 dances to music played by the Peerless Entertainers. A specialty dance called the "Black Bottom" was demonstrated by Marjorie MacCallum.[13]

Scotsburn was home to the county's first Women's Institute. The group organized cooking demonstrations, literary discussion papers, Red Cross work and garden parties. The 4-H movement started in 1924, when 16 youth joined the Mayflower Swine club at Central Caribou. Known as Boys and Girls Clubs, with the goal of educating farmers of the future, clubs came together in other rural areas, such as Bayview's Garden and Poultry Club (1928), Hopewell Guernsey Calf and Feeding Club (1930) and McLellan's Brook Garment Club. The only Black Girl Guide group in Canada formed in New Glasgow in the 1930s. Boy Scouts were especially appreciated for their Christmas Eve visits, when they would arrive at needy homes with toys they had collected and cleaned up. Youth groups could now enjoy summer camps opened along the Northumberland shore, in particular the Girl Guide camp given in memory of Rose Jette Goodman, who died in an air crash while training during World War II.

The bands and many amateur musicians displayed their talents onstage at shows, concerts and later on at music festivals. Thorburn Band. From left, front: [unknown], [unknown], William Brennan, George Poulain. Back row: *Harry Cameron, Tom Barclay, James H. Fraser, Nelson Wilson, Bert Fraser, [unknown], [unknown], Donald B. MacDonald, James Ellsworth, James Grant, Richard Cholmondeley.*

Melmerby Beach (A New Glasgow Resort), Little Harbour, Nova Scotia - 3

Soaking up the sun and sea at Melmerby Beach.

Lodges were still popular. In 1925, the Rotary Club in New Glasgow enjoyed an address on the mineral resources of Nova Scotia while the Gyro Club under Dr. Weldon Fraser was admitted to the Gyro International. The Rebekahs held a card party at the IOOF home in Pictou. Local councils of women were organized, and the IODE began in 1934. The object of the New Glasgow Horticultural Society was to interest and assist citizens in beautifying their immediate surroundings, to provide lectures on horticulture, and to hold garden competitions and flower shows. Of special interest to the community of dog fanciers, in September 1921 Mrs. James T. Fraser's Boston Terrier, Glow, won three firsts and a cup at the Saint John kennel show.

People enjoyed church organizations and outings, like Second Baptist's picnics at Pictou Landing. Throughout the day they swam and played games. After supper they "took out the guitars," remembers Catherine Shepherd Clark. "The dances we did were the foxtrot, sometimes the waltz, and the Charleston. Before going home we would pick a bucket of blueberries and dig clams. Then we would build a little fire in the backyard and cook the clams in a big pot. We also held picnics in town, in the field where the YMCA stands now. Everyone and his dog prepared for weeks. The food — roasts, salmon, tons of canned goods, cakes with sky high icing — and how the kids used to

Float all dressed for the Trenton parade

Green Hill Look-Off, Pictou County, Nova Scotia.

New Glasgow Rebekah Lodge Top row: *Miss E. Stewart, Miss C. Maynard, Mrs. A.W. MacDonald, Mrs. J.S. Fraser, Mrs. J. MacMillan, Mrs. W. Conrod.* 2nd row: *Mrs. B. MacMillan, Miss M. Munro, Miss S. Patton, Miss J., Munro, Mrs. Don Chisholm, Mrs. Wm. McKenzie, Miss G. McLaren, Mrs. A. Archibald.* 3rd row: *Mr.s D. Cumming, Mrs. Geo Munro, Mrs. S.R. Mackay, Mrs. Gus Arthur, Miss A.S. Fraser, Miss J. MacDonald, Mrs. D.C. Fraser, Miss Eva McLean, Mrs. Ed. Johnston, Mrs. McG. McLeod.* Front row: *Miss J. Fraser, Mrs. Geo. Fraser, Miss E. MacDonald, Mrs. Thomas Arthur.*

sneak up behind the committee and swipe some of the tasty morsels. It was quite the thing. Because we had a men's ball team and a women's ball team, we would have people coming from Truro, and sometimes Halifax."[14]

Church remained important in most people's lives. In 1925, the United Church was formed of the Presbyterian, Methodist and Congregational faiths, although many Presbyterians rejected union. Among the newer churches were Seventh Day Adventists who were offering "Back to the Bible" meetings in May 1928, the Church of the Nazarene who came to Trenton and a Pentecostal Assembly to New Glasgow.

Socializing centred around the home, where children warmed themselves with cocoa after coasting, or adults gathered to talk, play cards and maybe have a smoke. After all, MacDonald's advertised their chewing and smoking tobacco as "the tobacco with a heart."[15] Robert Hoegg remembers that around 1928 he first saw a woman smoking — an American tourist in a car at the Intervale. He ran home to tell his mother.[16]

Electric lights and central heating made homes more

Mi'kmaqs join in "Hector" celebrations, including from Pictou Landing, at left: Chief Matthew Francis, with wife Anieres and daughter Marta. Behind: Chief Joe and Mrs. Louisa Julian of Truro. Front centre: P.E.I. Chief John Sark with his wife and grandson. Right: Jeremiah Lone-Cloud, alias Luxey, Halifax, and his wife Sarbet.

Waldron's Studio employed the most up-to-date photographic technology to capture these family treasures on film. The studio has identified, from left: *Family of Mrs. John Horne; Thomas C. Kennedy children (Dorothy and Everett); and George MacGregor's daughter.*

comfortable. The radio came to replace the hearth as people gathered round for news of other parts of the world and to enjoy radio drama.

There were no more early morning fires to kindle, no more scuttling coal and wood. Kettles and toasters meant folks could enjoy their tea and breakfast without waiting for the stove to heat up. Refrigerators did away with the dribbling ice box, putting the ice man out of business. The toil of housework was lightened with vacuum cleaners and electric irons; women agreed that the electric washing machine was a wonderful appliance.

However, as the advertisers used sanitation as the driving force in their message to buy the appliances, women reacted by filling their available time with cleaning. It was easier to clean, and "clean" was so desirable that they did three laundries a week instead of one, and they vacuumed every day.

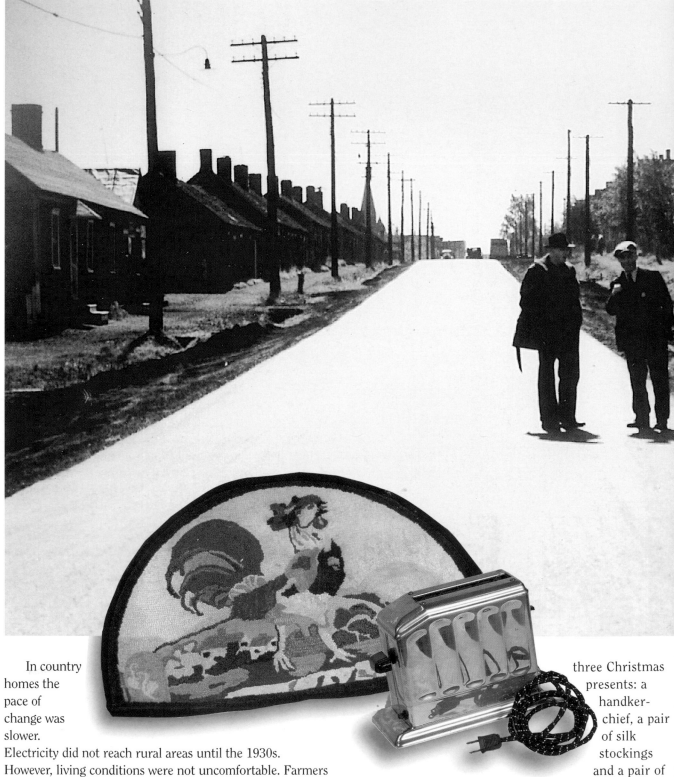

In country homes the pace of change was slower. Electricity did not reach rural areas until the 1930s. However, living conditions were not uncomfortable. Farmers were generally quite self-sufficient and contented themselves with what the conditions provided. The biggest obstacle was bad roads. Rural children missed school because of snow, ice, mud, inclement weather and farm work.

New conveniences were bought when people could afford them. In 1919, a farm woman recorded receiving three Christmas presents: a handkerchief, a pair of silk stockings and a pair of towels. Although an Eaton Beauty Doll was the dream of every little girl, often gifts were homemade, especially toys. Clothing was home-sewn and passed down from child to child.

Porridge, beans, and soup bones were food staples in many homes. Fruit and berries were preserved, as were

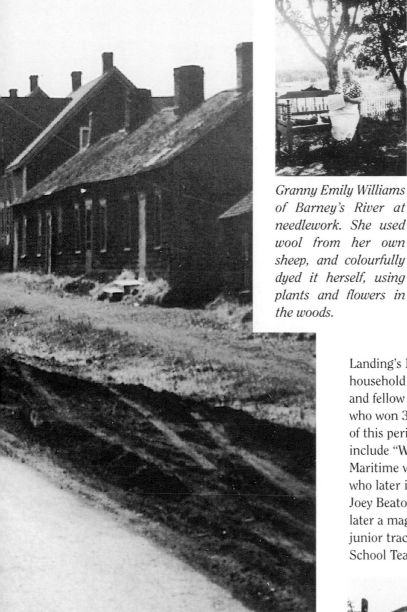

Granny Emily Williams of Barney's River at needlework. She used wool from her own sheep, and colourfully dyed it herself, using plants and flowers in the woods.

chants. Throughout the county it was customary when people were down on their luck for neighbours to bring a food basket. Stories abound about hard times during the Depression — eating blueberries to survive, digging ditches for a meagre welfare order, children going without shoes before snow was off the ground. Catherine Clark tells of selling berries and flowers door-to-door to get money for her school books.[18] When fathers had no work, many young girls scrubbed and cooked in middle-class homes to bring home money.

Sports were a favourite community pastime. During the 1930s both hockey and curling clubs in the county won provincial titles and softball became popular at this time. Strongman Chalmers Bigney of River John entertained with weight-lifting. Road racing made Pictou Landing's Noel Paul and Greenwood miner Roy Oliver household names. Oliver succeeded Westville marathoner and fellow Nova Scotia Hall of Famer Jimmy Hawboldt, who won 38 of his 55 races. Some other Pictonian athletes of this period recognized in the Sport Heritage Centre Hall include "Westville Windmill" Bobby Allan, a two-fisted Maritime welter boxing champ, boxing referee Bob Beaton, who later introduced the three judge system, hockey stars Joey Beaton and Foster "Moxie" Dixon, baseball pitcher, later a magistrate, Billie Richardson, and 1937 Canadian junior track and field champs, the New Glasgow High School Team, coached by Harold Smith.[19]

Acadia Coal housing, North Foord Street, Stellarton

vegetables from backyard plots. Hunting and fishing also provided food for the table. Zoning did not prohibit livestock in town, and many families tied a cow in the backyard and kept a few chickens. In 1921, the press reported that Thomas Cantley imported a pair of goats of a breed that was popular in British Columbia. A man who lived near Cantley's stone mansion remarked: "I haven't seen the goats, but I *smelled them*."[17]

Hardship was not uncommon, and mine disasters and labour problems accustomed people to pull together. During the 1925 strike, for example, miners served soup made of ingredients donated by local farmers and mer-

Moose hunting, believed to be near St. Paul's

As hard training was considered unhealthy and unfeminine, women were mostly limited to tennis, curling, swimming and skating, as well as some team sports such as church ball teams.

Bluenose Curlers, winner of the MacLellan Cup in 1935. From left, back: O.R. Fraser, J.A. Caldwell, R.B. Stewart, H.F. McNaughton. Front: Warren F. Lockhart, J.H. Murray, H.G. Grant, Mert McKenzie.

Maritime Sport Stars On Parade --- No. 4

BILLIE RICHARDSON IS RATED AS THE GREATEST PITCHER EVER DEVELOPED IN NOVA SCOTIA

RICHARDSON IS NOW MAGISTRATE IN STELLARTON

PITCHING FOR WESTVILLE IN 1921 AGAINST STELLARTON HE PERFORMED THE REMARKABLE FEAT OF STRIKING OUT 22 OF THE OPPOSING BATTERS IN ONE GAME.

RICHARDSON TOOK UP CURLING TWO YEARS AGO AND THEY SAY HE CAN DELIVER THE CURLING STONE LIKE HE DELIVERS THE OLD APPLE IN BASEBALL

CHAMBERS/'37

From left: *John MacCormack, Vernon MacDonald, Herb Mills, Murray McLeod, Bob MacDonald, Lawson Smith, Bill Moore. Back: Coach, Harold W. Smith*

World War II

While World War II brought renewed industrial activity, full employment and a prospering economy, it also brought a lot of anxiety about those who sailed overseas. The county militia, which had been training regularly

At Pictou, November 1939, from left: *Gerald MacDonald, Morrison, Dalton.*

between the two wars, enlisted. Pictou Highlanders served overseas with distinction, some as members of the North Nova Highlanders and others as West Novas. Many Pictonians enlisted, including twenty Blacks from New Glasgow who enlisted in the now unsegregated army. Others joined the Royal Canadian Air Force, the navy, and the medical corps. Some were paratroopers with the Black Devils. Many worked in the merchant marine ferrying vital supplies across the Atlantic. War memorials in the county indicate that 241 Pictonians gave their lives in the war.

Memorial tribute to Lt. J. Clifford Fraser, M.C., killed in Italy, March 1945.

Providing support at home, people bought war bonds and organized circles to sew and knit for servicemen. Christmas boxes were packed and sent. Rationing of food and gasoline at home was a small sacrifice at home to preserve freedom for future generations.

Dutch submarine used for Canadian naval training, repaired in Pictou during the war. Queen Wilhelmina visited when she was in the county and was presented with a miniature of the submarine by its crew.

CHAPTER 5

Modern perspectives

1945-1995

The post-war years in Pictou County included a period of prosperity followed by rapid change and, in some industrial sectors, stagnation. However, new business attracted to the area has brought diversity, while tourism built around Pictou's unique historical association with Scotland has expanded business opportunities in the major towns in the county.

Post-industrial economy

Unlike after World War I, Canada's industrial economy did not go into depression in 1945. This was largely because of a shortage of manufactured goods. For several years people had to put their names on a list to buy cars and appliances.

In Pictou County, coal mining, steel production and ship construction began the period strongly. For coal, however, that would soon change. Demand for the fuel encouraged DOSCO to open the first all-mechanized mine in Canada. Thorburn's McBean sharply contrasted with the old-fashioned pits at Stellarton and Westville, where tangled and highly combustible coal seams precluded electricity and mechanization. Modernization denied them, the old mines had become inefficient and unprofitable,

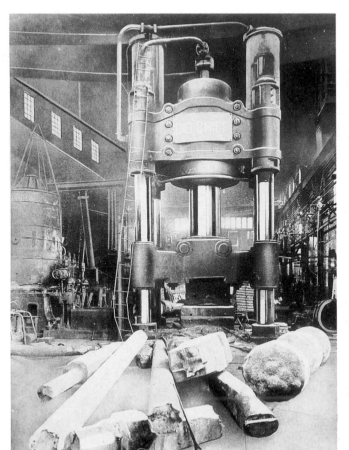

Old "Big Chief" forging press

New Forging process: steel ingot arrives at Trenton in its "hot box"

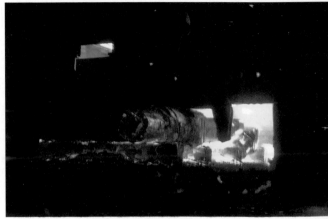

Heating the ingot back to temperature

just as coal found itself pushed out of the market by oil. In 1951, three spontaneous fires at the same time closed the Allan mine. When the Albion was worked out, and the MacGregor was closed by fire in 1957, there was no incentive for new development. Even though the Nova Scotia Power Commission's thermal power plant at Trenton burned local coal, the McBean was kept alive with subsidies until it was shut down in 1972. All that remained of the industry was the small Drummond mine, which closed in 1984. After 150 years of mining, it seemed as if a chapter in history had been closed.

Those last years were not without tragedy. Nineteen colliers were killed in the MacGregor mine in 1952. Pictonians may have been happy to put the grim side of mining behind them and consider coal mining finished. However, high oil prices and unemployment helped excite interest in the rich Foord seam. A proposal to sink a mine into the seam at Plymouth was approved although it was a controversial project, for safety and financial reasons. Curragh

Workers at Eastern Car

Resources Ltd.'s Westray mine, which incorporated the most modern mining technology, reached the coal in April, 1991. Less than one year later, on May 9, 1992, a methane explosion triggered a massive coal dust explosion. Despite an heroic rescue attempt, no survivors of the 26 men underground were found, and 11 bodies had to be left unrecovered.

In November 1994, in the largest civilian investiture ceremony ever, at Stellarton Governor General Ramon Hnatyshyn presented 96 medals of bravery to draegermen and bare-faced rescuers. The award was a long overdue recognition of the valour of mine rescue workers. Experts have recommended against ever reopening Westray. Meanwhile, strip mining, which started at Westville in the early 1980s, was reviewed in 1995 for Stellarton and Thorburn.

Overall, industry at Trenton can today be considered a success story, particularly the car works. In 1951, their second best year to date, Eastern Car shipped 2,602 cars to both foreign and domestic customers; the new business led to a 20,000 square-foot

The forging process

John Robison, front, *and Ed Bronson building the Dartmouth ferry at Pictou Foundries.*

Meanwhile in shipbuilding, Pictou Foundries took over Foundation Maritime after the war, and in 1953 consolidated into Fergusons' Industries. The first ship they built was a Dartmouth ferry. When the company was sold in 1974 to H.B. Nickerson, it had constructed 110 vessels. In 1995 the historic shipyard was closed. Its last major job was the construction of the *Confederation*, a 200-car ferry for the Caribou-Wood Islands route.

extension. During the 1960s the car works did a steady business, though the wheel foundry was closed. Almost every kind of railway freight car has been built at Trenton. During the 1970s and 1980s, business was punctuated with lay-offs, but by the mid-1990s prospects looked good for the future.

The other successful component of Trenton Works has been its steel forging plant. In 1951 the 55,000 axles it produced exceeded the 1948 record by over 10 percent. Shortly after, the plant modernized with the country's largest forging press. The machine shop and press could produce forgings up to 80 tons, a feat almost unequalled in the world. For the tensile strength needed in the shaft of naval destroyers, the steel had to be forged while still hot from its first pouring. A special insulated box to carry a newly poured ingot the 160 miles from Sydney Steel was invented. When the red hot ingot was unpackaged at Trenton it was heated still further, then forged and lathed. The process came to be applied to a diversity of large scale steel forgings.[1] Today this plant specializes in turbine forgings for generators. Both the car and forge operations are owned by Greenbriar, an Oregon company.

The third plant at Trenton, Trenton Industries, converted from gun manufacture to maintenance work for Eastern Car. They built the DOSCO continuous miner, and also manufactured brewing and dairy equipment before closing in the 1970s.

This period has seen a consolidation in the forest industry. As late as 1965 the county had 32 lumber producers. Among them was Westville's Trueman Matheson who invented a mechanical deal carrier for separating and piling lumber by width. In 1966 his mill shipped two million board feet of rough lumber to England. His mill folded at his death. "The Pictou County Community Profile" lists five mills in 1993, employing about 100 men and women, including the Williams' mill, successor to Dewars' Mills and furniture factory, which operated at Barney's River almost a century ago.

Other enterprises with roots in the industrial heyday — Maritime Steel and I. Matheson, for example — continue to operate. A sampling of new manufacturers who appeared over this period produced goods including paint, electronic parking meters, workplace clothing, hot tubs and leatherware.

Quality knives have been crafted by the late Rudolph Grohmann and his family since they found refuge at Pictou after fleeing the Sudatenland after World War II. A fabric artists' co-operative has been a venue for showcasing the work of craftspeople and artists.

Oscar Peterson advertises Clairtone stereos

Clairtone worker

Although small business is an integral part of the county economy, it could not replace the jobs lost in mining. Industrial Estates Ltd.(IEL) and the Pictou County Research and Development Corporation (PICORD) were challenged to find new industry. Through their efforts those employed in manufacturing increased by 71 percent to 4,500 people between 1961 and 1966.

The first firm to come to Pictou County was Donato, Faini and Figli. The Italian firm knitted clothing in all shades of the rainbow, much of which was sold in Europe and New York. The factory's outlet store dressed the county in quality knitwear. The company, whose 100 employees were mostly women, closed in 1972 when the owner died.

In 1966 Royal Typewriter transferred twenty employees from Montreal and hired sixty-five locally. The company was predicted to eventually employ 1,500 people. But trucks suddenly began carting off equipment, and with it, promises of employment. Optimism prevailed, and at the official opening of Clairtone Sound, Premier Stanfield extolled: "Today there is a new and revitalized Pictou County... We see it in ship-building, in construction, in boxcars; we see it in apartments, homes, motels, offices, and a hospital. We see it at nearby Abercrombie and we see it dramatically in this very building."

Clairtone opened in Stellarton in 1966, with $3.5 million of provincial and federal funds, and an employment potential of 700. The TV production line was automated and computer-programmed. VIPs enjoyed an opening reception on wheels as a special nine-car train brought them from the airport. Minister without Portfolio, and later Prime Minister, John N. Turner participated in the ceremony at the Stellarton Industrial Park, a stone's throw from where his mother was born in a coal company house. Clairtone President Peter Munk predicted Nova Scotia was on the brink of an industrial revolution. He paid tribute to a workforce "able to be trained in a short time to take over work with the complicated machinery. The human asset will make this area grow. Clairtone will never let you down." [2] High hopes, for although the firm produced superior products, market and business failings forced it to close in 1972.

However, Scott Paper's pulp mill at Abercrombie brought new vitality. When the wind blows across the water Pictonians pragmatically call the smell from the mill "prosperity." Important as the mill has been economically, environmentally it has left a festering sore. The provincial government took responsibility for effluent, purchasing Mi'kmaq land at Boat Harbour for its discharge. The site turned into a stinking cesspool, while the effluent killed

A mere memory are the days when young women arrived from New Brunswick and the Magdalenes, looking poor and malnourished, but after a week or two in Caribou in the Maritime Packers' bunkhouses, and with their first pay in their pockets, they perked up. On Saturday night, Pictou came alive when they came for a night on the town. Local schoolgirls also worked vacations at the canneries. Anne Boone of Braeshore recalled her job was to feed the small feeler claws through a hand wringer to extract the meat.

plant and animal life. After a lawsuit, the Mi'kmaqs were financially compensated, but the effluent problem remains unresolved. In 1995, Scott Paper was bought by Kimberly Clark Corporation.

The second company to arrive in recent years is now the county's largest employer. Michelin Tire opened in October 1971 in Granton, and has since opened two more plants in Nova Scotia. In 1993, Michelin had 1900 people on its payroll.

Food processing, most notably in lobster and dairy products, is ongoing. In 1991, fish landings represented a value of $6,757,000, second only to manufacturing at $470,875,000. Lobster is now sold fresh, and the days of canning are over. Today only one cannery, the Lismore Seafood Company processes lobster, in cold packs and in brine. The plant, which employs 100 in peak season, also packs herring roe for Japan. Scallops, herring and mackerel represent most of the remainder of sea landings. For several years, in September beaches near Toney River were busy with Irish moss harvesters, but the plant there was closed.

By 1967 only 15 percent of the county's population lived on farms. The East River used to be humming with working farms all the way to Sunny Brae. Now, the farm as an institution is threatened. Many rural houses have been torn down or are deserted, while others are empty during the day, their residents at work in manufacturing. In 1991 the county had 383 farms occupying over 88,479 acres.

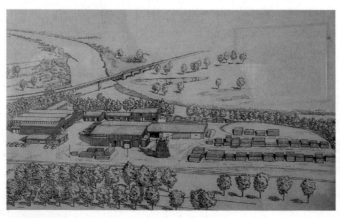

D. Porter and Son's lumber mill, Stellarton

Scott Paper Ltd.'s pulp mill, Abercrombie

Crops included vegetables and grains, hay being predominant. Livestock reflected a renewed interest in lamb, but included beef and dairy cattle as well.

Scotsburn Cooperative Dairy has been the predominant processor of farm products. After the war the company expanded to farm supply, cold storage and ice cream making, and in 1966 they merged with the local dairies of Allen's and Stevenson's. They have since expanded their product line and acquired facilities elsewhere in the province.

Sobeys became the major grocery retailer after they bought Barkers' grocery chain, opened self-serve supermarkets and expanded throughout the Maritimes. From its roots as a small butcher shop, Sobeys is now part of Empire Company, a food and pharmaceutical distribution and retailing firm with head office in Stellarton.

Today, business in the county is well-served by the Pictou Regional Development Commission which encourages business retention and growth, with the aim of consolidating Pictou County as a leading commercial and industrial area in Atlantic Canada.

One important asset is the area's transportation links. On June 30, 1966, Mayor William Sobey of Stellarton threw the switch for the county's first traffic lights. That same year a causeway opened from Abercrombie to Pictou, cutting many miles off the road trip from up-river towns.

Now, the Trans-Canada Highway makes long-distance car travel more efficient and comfortable, and passenger train service has disappeared.

Although Pictou Harbour is no longer as busy as it once was, the value of cargo — kraft pulp produced by Scott Paper and hardwood bound for Europe — exported through the port is greater than ever before. Shipping terminated from Pictou Landing by 1955, and the ferry to Pictou stopped five years later. In the early 1970s the SS *Lovatt*'s twice weekly freight and passenger run to the Magdalene Islands ended. Seasonal car ferry service continues to run between Caribou and Prince Edward Island. Passenger airline service was offered at Trenton for a few years, until traffic proved insufficient. Access to international air travel is less than two hours away by car, and after only five hours of flight a Pictonian can set foot in Scotland — a far cry from the 11-week voyage of the *Hector*, 220 years ago.

The Ashagola *ferried up to five cars and passengers from Pictou Landing to Pictou, eight times a day.*

At home

Pictou County is home to many people whose roots go back several generations. At Pictou Landing, descendants of the original inhabitants still make their homes. Government attempted to centralize Mi'kmaqs in 1942, but local residents who relocated to Shubenacadie soon came back after inferior construction rendered their housing unhabitable. In 1960 band holdings increased with the granting of Wooley and Indian Islands in Merigomish Harbour. At their registered heritage church of St. Anne's, Mi'kmaqs observe a day of service and ceremony every July.

Door-to-door selling faded after the 1951 Indian Act institutionalized welfare. Mi'kmaq Jenny Stevens regrets how this also took away the incentive to hunt and pick berries; instead, a diet of processed foods is today reflected in health problems for older Mi'kmaqs. After being denied human and civil rights for 200 years, the aboriginals have become more confident in their demands for treaty rights, while many have returned to creating traditional crafts.

In 1946 Halifax hairdresser Viola Desmond drew attention to racism in the county when she went to an evening movie at the Roseland. During the day, the cinema permitted Blacks downstairs, but at night they had to sit in the balcony. When she refused to move upstairs, she was arrested, spent the night in jail and fined $25 for failing to pay 19 cents amusement tax — the difference between up and down tickets.

The incident, reported in *Time* magazine, was a catalyst in the fight against racism.

At the time Blacks were welcome in only Chinese restaurants and, at best, might receive counter, but not table service in other eateries. To improve race relations, in 1946 Carrie Best started Nova Scotia's first Black newspaper *The Clarion*, later renamed The *Negro Citizen*. Best has been awarded the Order of Canada and an honourary doctorate for her fight against racism.

About 1965, with similar goals, an organization of Blacks and Whites called the Pursuers, went door-to-door inquiring of stores why they never saw Blacks working there. Gradually, through their efforts, and through young people demanding equality, prejudice against Blacks declined.

Sally Sark, a popular Mi'kmaq woman who sold door-to-door, here wearing her wedding hat.

In 1949 the county welcomed the largest single group of immigrants since Scots in the 1800s. John Soosar remembers, "it was teeming," that October night when a train carrying thirty-seven Estonians steamed into Hopewell. Despite the rain, a crowd turned out to greet these "Displaced Persons" from camps in Germany. David Wilson of Marshdale, who had worked with United Nations refugee relief, had initiated the setting up of an Estonian handicraft colony. In fields of muck, the refugees happily unloaded their possessions into the small cabins Wilson had put up on his farm. They represented a home, freedom, for many who had been in flight since Russia occupied their country in 1941. Though few spoke English, the dinner put on by the community that night in the Wilsons' kitchen was a warm, companionable event.[3]

In all, Wilson brought in ninety refugees, including Latvians and Lithuanians. Over the winter the county responded with an outpouring of generosity, donating Christmas baskets, food, clothing and furnishings.

The newcomers lived at Marshdale at least one winter, during which the children learned English at the farm-

Estonian refugees being entertained by I.O.D.E. women include some who stayed in Pictou County: front left: Jaan Soosar; behind Jaan: Mati Maelde and Peep Maelde; Rein Ulesoo (small boy in sailor collar); back row, third from left: Loreida Ulesoo.

Sunny Brae

New Glasgow, when main streets were alive

house of retired teacher, Annie Crockett, before starting school. Eventually most of the group moved to central Canada to find work. The handicraft colony was not successful as their exquisite, labour-intensive inlaid wood crafts were too expensive for the market. Some families stayed and enriched the cultural mosaic of Pictou County.

After the war came general improvement along with rationalization of living conditions. When sewers were put into the mining areas, honey carts were retired. New efficient ranch-style houses reflected the design philosophy that house should serve the needs of its occupants. Compact kitchens were activity-driven, with built-in cupboards and counters. The demise of the kitchen couch reflected the end of the kitchen as a gathering place. Informal entertaining moved to the new basement recreation room.

Development went on in urban areas, spurred by the industrial activity of the 1960s. The *Evening News* of August 9, 1966 announced plans for twenty-four new bungalows at Victory Heights in Pictou. New Glasgow's west side was expanding, while in the growing south end of Stellarton, Valley Woods was introduced as a new upscale housing development. Meanwhile, main streets declined in favour of shopping centres like the Aberdeen, Highland, and West Side, which attracted franchise and chain stores, putting local firms out of business. Of significance was the closing of Goodmans's in 1985, which had clothed the county since 1904.

Local broadcasting came in 1953 with CKEC radio station, and before many years satellites were beaming in television. Cable television introduced community programming.

The county continued to update its health care facilities. March 30, 1955, was moving day for the Aberdeen Hospital. Patients were moved from the old to the new facility in a convoy of several ambulances, station wagons, and private cars. In 1969, Glen Haven Manor began as a nursing home for the county's aged, as senior citizens' housing was also becoming a municipal priority.

By 1957 Progressive Conservatives had assumed power in both Ottawa and Halifax. Russell McEwan was a popular Conservative MP from Pictou County for sixteen years. His successor, Elmer McKay held the seat until 1993, except for one year when he resigned to allow Brian Mulroney, the Opposition Leader, to enter Parliament on a by-election. He

Champion Scottish dancer Deborah Robson of Stellarton won medals in international competition.

regained the seat in 1984. After 36 years as a Tory seat, Central Nova was won by Liberal Roseanne Skoke in 1993.

Three electoral districts return members to the provincial legislature. In Pictou West and Pictou Centre, Conservatives have held sway since 1949, represented by Donald R. MacLeod, Harvey Veniot, Jack MaIsaac, Dr. John Hamm and Donald McInnes, and with two Liberal interludes from Ralph Fiske and Daniel Reid. In Pictou East A. Lloyd MacDonald was succeeded by Donald Cameron who was Premier of the province in 1992-3. After Cameron's resignation, Liberal Wayne Fraser took the seat.

During the first half of this period, the nuclear family was the status quo. Government used income tax incentives to prod women, who had worked during the war in business and industry, to return to the home. This was portrayed as an act of patriotism when hundreds of delisted men were seeking work. As the average wage for the male breadwinner doubled over the 1950s, the quality of family life improved. Many parents of "baby boomers", wanting to give their children opportunities they never had, took advantage of various activities available to enrich youthful lives. Parents made sacrifices to pay for private lessons in piano, highland dancing, and figure skating. Churches offered youth groups for all ages; the boy scouts had high profile with annual skating meets and jamborees. In 1965, Stellarton Air Cadets were named best squadron in Canada. Through their schools, students enjoyed sports and public speaking events, while Allied Youth hearkened back to the temperance zeal of their grandparents.

Rural youth moved from their country schoolhouses to the new central high schools of East Pictou (opened in 1952), and West Pictou (1960). During the 1960s Catholic schools closed, or were taken over by the public system. The Pictou County Vocational School was built at Birch Hill in 1962. It is somehow fitting that as the traditional industry of mining ended, the technical and trades school opened on the site of the home of the first manager of Acadia Coal. The school has since been reorganized as a community college. Since 1946 a Fisheries School at Pictou has offered a variety of programs from gear and navigation through to aquaculture. By the mid-1960s government-sponsored student loans became a great equalizer by allowing children of less means to pursue post-secondary education.

Meanwhile, the eight-hour workday released more time for enjoyment. In the 1950s, Saturday night entertainment included a movie at the Highland Drive-in. With the arrival of television, however, overall movie attendance declined, forcing some cinemas to close. As television kept people home, it decreased sociability. They visited less; and the age-old pastimes of telling stories and making kitchen music together faded away.

Organized music, however, remained a dynamic force in the county. New Glasgow's Ceilidh was the first girls' pipe band. It was followed by the Balmoral, Dunvegan and Heatherbells. On June 4, 1962, the Stellarton Air Cadets Fife and Drum Band gave their first performance. Maintaining their musical tradition, Second Baptist Church's Step-a-Head-Male Chorus, Pleasure Singers and Mixed Chorus sang spiritual vocals throughout the Maritimes into the 1950s. "Woman Trouble" was a popular musical put on by the Kiwanis Club. Both travelling and local shows have performed over the years at the modern venue of the deCoste Centre in Pictou. The Royal Swingsters and George Condon band are remembered for their music at grown-up dances, while during the 1950s and 1960s school auditoriums and IOOF halls shuddered, along with parents, to the beat of the Blue Cats, Atomics,

Chevelles and Strangerz.

Epitomizing the quality of choral singing is the Pictou District Junior Honour Choir's performance in May 1995 at Carnegie Hall, New York. The 57th Annual Music Festival held in April 1995 was the venue for the many talented individual and group musicians to shine.

Horse racing, once a popular sport, has died out. When the Blue Acres track opened in the summer of 1946, Betty Bud, driven by Sample of Charlottetown, won the inaugural race. The stake paid out $3400 plus $50 to the driver and $10 to the groom. When the track closed just six years later it had hosted a variety of events from a five-ring circus to a Gaelic Mod. Racing continued at Parkdale's Union oval for several more years.

Of teams, the most celebrated was the Stellarton Albions. As part of the Halifax and District League, the local and imported baseball players won several championships during the 1950s. The club "was run on a grand scale" that included professional umpires brought in from the States, groundskeeper, laundry service, and two grandstands with press box and broadcasting booth.[4] "Stellarton's Golden Decade of Baseball" ended when the Albions dropped out of the expensive league in 1958. However, the Albions continued to fare well as members with Westville, New Glasgow

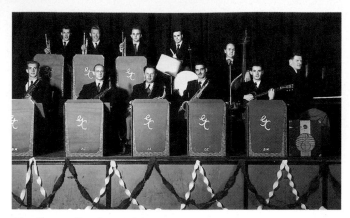

The George Condon orchestra

and Antigonish in the Pictou Twilight Baseball League.

The inaugural issue of *The Nova Scotia Sports Heritage Centre* says Robert "Tic" Williams was "perhaps gifted with greater natural skill than any player produced in the Maritimes." Although a native of Charlottetown, Tic spent most of his career in Pictou, where after 1944 he "terrorized the APC League, winning the scoring title nine successive times." Thorburn's Lowell MacDonald, who went on to the NHL, was a hockey star at East Pictou Rural High.

Early in this period several women's softball teams competed in the county, and New Glasgow High had a girls' hockey team. By the 1960s soccer, basketball, volleyball and track and field were standard girls' sports in schools.

Many boys got their start boxing in neighbourhood rings, like Russell "Sparky" Paris's boxing club in the Vale Road area. The county's most famous boxer was Art Hafey, who was once ranked the world's number one featherweight contender. Hafey is honoured in Nova Scotia's Sports Hall of Fame, along with the man who promoted his matches, Harry Trainor of New Glasgow. For several years the Johnny Miles Marathon has been an annual event, with local runners consistently among the winners.

For several years recreational sailors enjoyed their Royal William facility at Pictou Landing. Indulging the county's famous sociability are bowling leagues, and golf and curling clubs. After being dormant for fifty years, the YMCA reopened with a pool in 1971. Trenton Steeltown Centennial Park's campground and family swimming pool is enjoyed by Pictonians and tourists alike.

Luckily, the weather usually obliges for the summer rite of soaking up sun and sea on the forty miles of beaches, and for the profusion of summer festivals that celebrate the heritage of Pictou County: Westville's Canada Day party, the Ceilidh at Hopewell's historic swinging bridge, the Lyons' Brook Betsey landing reenactment all evoke patriotism. Ex-patriots have laughed with old friends at Stellarton's Homecoming Week, New Glasgow's Black Reunion, and the

Norman Leroy "Patty" Lawrence of New Glasgow won many titles in the world of army boxing. He is shown here prior to winning the Army Open Middleweight Championship in 1959 at age 23.

East Pictou Rural Fair. Or, they have sought out their roots at the geneological centre located in the former home of the Rev. Thomas McCulloch. Villages from River John to Sunny Brae have served up home-cooked local specialties at lobster suppers, strawberry socials, and chowder challenges.

The Scottish heritage, celebrated in clan reunions, and over several days of highland games, music and dancing at New Glasgow's Festival of the Tartans, has been maintained as a primary focus for tourism. Trap hauling and scallop shucking contests have enlivened the Lobster Carnival, alongside the Northumberland Fisheries Museum where the Silver Bullet, a lobster boat which won three consecutive Carnival races has been on display. The Pictou North-Colchester Exhibition has showcased farm and 4-H achievements. Accompanying many of these festivals were parades, and the Bill Lynch show, where, to the surprised recognition of many, in the mid 1960s a Stellarton girl lit up the stage as Electric Lady.

As well as festivals, the county boasts several sites that reflect its culture. Together, they have been important as an economic as well as a social force. Through showcasing their heritage, particularly over the summer months, the county has succeeded in attracting more tourists for longer stays, at the same time as giving Pictonians an appreciation of their roots. Recently opened was the Museum of Industry on the site of the old Foord pit, the New Glasgow Firefighters'

Parade during the Hector celebrations in front of the Hector Heritage Quay, Pictou.

Museum, and a Sports Hall of Fame. On the Pictou waterfront a new quay and marina was opened with a replica of the *Hector* under construction. These attractions complemented the historic treasures on display at the

Carmichael/Stewart houses, the Burning Bush Museum, and restored sites like the Loch Broom church and McPherson's Mill. Pictou County has melded its wealth of history and its traditional hospitality into an economic, and cultural resource. Much appreciation for recording this past is accorded to county historian James M. Cameron, who died in 1995.

Over half a century, society has changed considerably. Mothers are in the paid workforce, and the definition of family has loosened to include single parents, same-sex unions, and "mergers" resulting from second marriages. Even though society was no longer straitjacketed by traditional structures, the values that distinguished Pictou County were and are as strong as ever. This was poignantly brought home by Governor General Hnatyshyn while presenting the Westray bravery medals. "Look around you, the faces you see are the faces of decent people," he said. He went on to extol the courage and compassion shown during the disaster, where everyone came together to help out — whether in food or financial donations, or in time, energy, or heroism. Pictou County exemplified, he said, "what is best about the human spirit."

What is best about the human spirit... When we look back over the centuries of development in Pictou County, no clause can better sum up the attitudes that built this part of the province. Settlers took a rough land and carved a settlement out of it, using the wealth of natural resources to sustain themselves. From their mistakes, they learned; upon their successes, they built. Concurrently, they established a society, enlightened in education, politics, and culture. Out of the long legacy of mining tragedies evolved compassion and charity. Whenever they were set back, Pictonians regrouped, seeking opportunity from outside, but also relying on their own natural and human resources. With such a heritage, Pictou County has remained a place we're proud to call home.

Marksmen of the Pictou County Rifle Association, John Thompson, above, and George Harper excelled for Canada at Bisley.

Endnotes

Chapter 1:

1. Pohl, Frederick J. *Atlantic Crossings Before Columbus*

2. Denys, Nicolas, *The Description and Natural History of the Coasts of North America* (Acadia)

3. Rand, S. T., *The History, Manners, Customs, Language, and Literature of the Micmac Tribe of Indians of Nova Scotia and P.E. Island*

4. Paul, Daniel N., *We Were Not the Savages*

5. Patterson, Rev. George, *A History of Pictou County*

6. Ibid.

7. MacLaren, George, *The Pictou Book: Stories of Our Past*

8. Patterson

9. Ibid.

10. MacKay, John, Esquire, "Reminiscences of a Long Life"

11. Patterson

12. Ibid.

13. MacLaren

14. Patterson, from MacGregor's diary

15. MacKay

16. Ibid.

17. Ibid.

18. Ibid.

19. Cameron, James M., *The Ships, Shipbuilders and Seamen of Pictou County*

20. Patterson

21. Ibid.

22. Ibid.

23. MacKay

24. Patterson

25. Ibid.

26. Ibid.

27. Ibid.

28. Ibid.

29. MacKay

30. Patterson

Chapter 2:

1. Cameron, James M., *The Ships, Shipbuilders and Seamen of Pictou County*

2. Public Archives of Nova Scotia, RG5 Series GP, Vol.13.

3. Ryan, Judith, "A History of Railway Development in Nova Scotia," N.S. Museum of Industry report.

4. Rand, S. T., *The History, Manners, Customs, Language, and Literature of the Micmac Tribe of Indians of Nova Scotia and P.E. Island*

5. Ibid.

6. Patterson, Rev. George, *A History of Pictou County*

7. Howe, Joseph, *Western and Eastern Rambles: Travel Sketches of Nova Scotia*, edited by M.G. Parks

8. Ibid.

9. Barry, James, Diaries 1849-1919 (List is a composite)

10. Ibid.

11. *Eastern Chronicle*, assorted issues October-December 1866

12. Howe

13. Patterson

14. Howe

Chapter 3:

1.Barrett, Peter, Twelve Years in North America, Public Archives of Nova Scotia (PANS) MG1, Vol. 3196A.

2. *Our Dominion*. Historical Publishing Company of Canada, 1887

3. Calder, Frank W., *History and Stories of Springville, Pictou County, Nova Scotia*

4. Cameron, James M., *Pictou County's History*

5. Nova Scotia's Industrial Centre. Issued under the approval of the Councils of New Glasgow, Stellarton, Westville, and Trenton, 1916.

6. *Our Dominion*

7. *Eastern Chronicle*, July 28, 1883

8. Nova Scotia's Industrial Centre, 1916

9. *Our Dominion*

10. Nova Scotia's Industrial Centre, 1916

11. Cameron, *Pictou County's History*.

12. Ibid.

13. Paul, Daniel, *We Were Not the Savages*.

14. Francis, Barry, "Pictou Landing Reserve: A History"

15. MacKay, John, Esquire, "Reminiscences of a Long Life."

16. *Our Dominion*

17. Ibid.

18. Ibid.

19. Ibid.

20. Ibid.

21. Ibid.

22. Ibid.

23. Ibid.

24. Ibid.

25. Ibid.

26. Ibid.

27. Ibid.

28. Ibid.

29. Barrett

30. *Our Dominion*

31. Ibid.

32. Sinclair, John H., "Letters to my Grandson"

33. Ibid.

34. Ibid.

35. Ibid.

36. Carmichael, Caroline, "Reflections on 80 Years of Life."

37. *Eastern Chronicle*, May 23, 1911

38. *Our Dominion*

39. Barrett.

40. Assorted issues, *Eastern Chronicle*, 1889-1891

41. Cameron, *Pictou County's History*

42. "Report on a Limited Survey of both Rural and Urban Conditions, The Pictou District", the Pictou Survey Committee by the Departments of Social Service and Evangelism of the Presbyterian and Methodist Churches, 1915

43. *Eastern Chronicle*, August 1916

44. Ibid. January 24, 1901.

45. Ryan, Judith, "Home Electrification," Nova Scotia Museum of Industry report

46. Ryan, Judith, "The Feminization of Office Labour in Nova Scotia," N.S. Museum of Industry report

47. Ibid.

48. McPhie, Rev. J.P., M.A., *Pictonians at Home and Abroad*

49. *Stellarton Star*, December 8, 1911

50. *Eastern Chronicle*, August 1883

51. Cameron, James M., *Pictonians in Arms*

52. *Pictou Advocate*, December, 1915

Chapter 4:

1. Cameron, James M., *Pictou County's History*

2. Author's research tapes

3. Barry Family Diaries, 1919

4. Ibid.

5. Conversation with Robert Hoegg, 1994

6. Ibid.

7. Assorted issues of *Evening News*, 1925-1926

8. Cameron, James M., *Political Pictonians*

9. *Eastern Chronicle*, August 21, 1933

10. Rose, Clifford, *Four Years With the Demon Rum*

11. MacIntyre, N. Carroll, *The Life and Adventures of Detective Peter Owen Carroll*

12. *Evening News*, November 11, 1925

13. Ibid., April 6, 1927

14. Conversation with Catherine Clark, 1994

15. *Evening News,* July 1920

16. Conversation with Robert Hoegg

17. *Eastern Chronicle*, September 2, 1921

18. Conversation with Catherine Clark

19. The Nova Scotia Sports Heritage Centre, Inaugural and 3rd Issues

Chapter 5:

1. Cameron, James M., *Pictou County's History*

2. *Evening News*, June 22, 1966

3. Conversation with John Soosar, 1994

4. From an anonymous private collection

Bibliography

"The Advocate Centennial," Pictou, N.S.: *The Pictou Advocate*, 1993.

Barrett, Peter, *Twelve Years in North America*, Public Archives of Nova Scotia (PANS) MG1, Vol. 3196A.

Barry, James, Diaries 1849-1919, PANS.

Best, Carrie M., *That Lonesome Road: The Autobiography of Carrie M. Best*, New Glasgow, N.S.: Clarion Publishing, 1977.

Buckner, P.A. & Frank, David, editors, "Atlantic Canada After Confederation," *The Acadiensis Reader:* Volume Two, Fredericton, N.B.: Acadiensis, 1985.

Calder, Frank W., *History and Stories of Springville Pictou County, Nova Scotia*, Hantsport, N.S.: Lancelot Press, 1992.

Cameron, James M., *A Century of Industry: The Story of Canada's Pioneer Steel Producer*, the Trenton Centennial Commission, Nova Scotia, 1983.

Cameron, James M., *More About Pictonians*, Hantsport, Nova Scotia: Lancelot Press, 1976.

Cameron, James M., *Pictonians in Arms*, Fredericton, N.B.: The University of New Brunswick and the Author, 1969.

Cameron, James M., *Pictou County's History*, New Glasgow: Pictou County Historical Society, 1972.

Cameron, James M., *Political Pictonians*, Ottawa: The Author, 1966.

Cameron, James M., *The Ships, Shipbuilders and Seamen of Pictou County*, New Glasgow: The Pictou County Historical Society, 1990.

Cameron, James M. *Still More About Pictonians*, Hantsport, Nova Scotia: Lancelot Press, 1985.

Cameron, James M. *Wreck of the Melmerby and other Pictou County Stories*, New Glasgow, N.S.: The Hector Publishing Co. Ltd., 1963.

Carmichael, Caroline, "Reflections on 80 Years of Life," unpublished article among the Sinclair family papers, 1932.

Denys, Nicolas, *The Description and Natural History of the Coasts of North America* (Acadia) Paris, France, 1672. Translated by William F. Ganong, Toronto: The Champlain Society, 1908.

Dorrington, Aubrey, *History of Stellarton*, Pictou, N. S.: The Advocate Printing and Publishing Co. Ltd., 1976.

Doull Scrapbook #8, PANS VF vol.9 #3.

Francis, Barry, "Pictou Landing Reserve: A History," unpublished paper.

The Letters of Charlotte Geddie and Charlotte Geddie Harrison, PANS V88#1.

Haliburton, Thomas Chandler, *An Historical and Statistical Account of Nova Scotia*, Halifax: Joseph Howe, Publisher, 1829.

Harvey, A.S., *the export base of the pictou county economy*, Halifax, Nova Scotia: The Institute of Public Affairs, Dalhousie University, 1968.

Hawkins, Marjorie; MacKenzie, Hector; MacQuarrie, John, *Gairloch, Pictou County, Nova Scotia*, 1977.

"History of Second Baptist Church," Second Baptist Church, New Glasgow.

Howe, Joseph, *Western and Eastern Rambles: Travel Sketches of Nova Scotia*, edited by M.G. Parks, Toronto: University of Toronto Press, 1973.

Kirincich, M. Stephen, *A Centennial History of Stellarton*, Antigonish, N.S.: Scotia Design Publications, 1990.

Kyte, Jack et al., *Native Born: A Brief History of the Black Presence in Pictou County*, Pictou, Scott Paper through Advocate Printing, 1990.

MacIntyre, N. Carroll, *The Life and Adventures of Detective Peter Owen Carroll*, Antigonish, Sundown Publications, 1985.

MacKay, John, Esquire, "Reminiscences of a Long Life," unpublished article among the Sinclair family papers. (MacKay's father was the last of the Hereditary Pipers to the MacKenzies of Gairloch, Scotland. His great-grandfather was blind, known as "Piobar Dall" or the "Blind Piper." He was also a poet, by the name of Angus MacKay.)

MacLaren, George, *Nova Scotia Glass*, Halifax, N.S., The Nova Scotia Museum, 1968.

MacLaren, George, *The Pictou Book: Stories of Our Past*, New Glasgow, N.S.: the Hector Publishing Company, 1954.

MacPhie, Rev. J.P., M.A., *Pictonians at Home and Abroad*, Boston, Massachusetts: Pinkham Press, 1914.

Matheson, Kezia, "The Dryden Murder," unpublished article.

Nova Scotia's Industrial Centre. Issued under the approval of the Councils of New Glasgow, Stellarton, Westville, and Trenton, 1916.

The Nova Scotia Sports Heritage Centre, Inaugural Issue, 1980.

The Nova Scotia Sports Heritage Centre, 3rd Issue, 1982.
Our Dominion, Toronto, Ontario: The Historical Publishing Company of Canada, 1887. PANS f129 07.

Patterson, Rev. George, *History of Pictou County*. Facsimile Edition. Belleville, Ontario: Mica Publishing, 1972. (Originally published in Montreal, Dawson and Sons, 1877.)

Paul, Daniel N., *We Were Not the Savages*, Halifax, N.S.: Nimbus Publishing, 1993.

Pelletier, Gaby, "The Micmac Dilemma At the End of the 17th Century," *Journal of the New Brunswick Museum*, 1980, pp 103-110.

Pictou County's 4-H, 1924-1984. (PANS).

Pictou County Community Profile, Pictou Regional Development Commission, 1993.

Pictou County: Leading entreprise into the future, Pictou Regional Development Commission, 1994.

Place Names and Places of Nova Scotia, Halifax, N.S.: the Public Archives of Nova Scotia, 1967.

Pohl, Frederick J. *Atlantic Crossings Before Columbus*, New York: W.W. Norton & Company, 1961.

"Report on a Limited Survey of both Rural and Urban Conditions, The Pictou District", prepared by the Pictou Survey Committee by the Departments of Social Service and Evangelism of the Presbyterian and Methodist Churces, 1915.

Public Archives of Nova Scotia, RG5 Series GP, Vol.13: Petitions to the Provincial Secretary for Patents.

Rand, S. T., *The History, Manners, Customs, Language, and Literature of the Micmac Tribe of Indians of Nova Scotia and P.E. Island*, Halifax: James Bowes & Son, 1850. PANS VF171 #5.

Rose, Clifford, *Four Years With the Demon Rum*, Fredericton N.B.: Acadiensis Press, 1980.

Ryan, Judith Hoegg, *Coal in Our Blood*, Halifax, N.S.: Formac Publishing, 1992.

Ryan, Judith, *Home Electrification*, 1993 research report for Nova Scotia Museum of Industry.

Ryan, Judith, *The Feminization of Office Labour in Nova Scotia*, 1992 research report for Nova Scotia Museum of Industry.

Ryan, Judith, *A History of Railway Development in Nova Scotia*, 1991 research report for Nova Scotia Museum of Industry.

Sandberg, L.A., *The Deindustrialization of Pictou County, Nova Scotia*, unpublished Phd. Thesis, McGill University, 1985.

Sherwood, Roland H., *Sagas of the Land and Sea*, Hantsport, N.S.: Lancelot Press, 1980.

Sinclair, John H., "Letters to my Grandson", unpublished paper among the Sinclair family papers.

Smith, H.I. and Wintemberg, W.J., *Some Shell-heaps in Nova Scotia*, Ottawa: King's Printer, 1929.

Westville Heritage Group and the Grade 12 English Class of Westville High School, *Celebrating Our Heritage: the History of Westville*, Westville, N.S.

Newspapers:
Colonial Patriot , December 7, 1827. *Mechanic & Farmer*, 1840. The *Stellarton Star* December 8, 1911. *Eastern Chronicle*, Various issues, 1866-1952. *Eastern Federationist*, pub by the Pictou County Trades and Labour council, May 31, 1919. *Evening News*, various issues 1920 - 1966. *Pictou Advocate*, various issues. *Colonial Standard* August 21, 1900.
Conversations and Personal Interviews.

Photo Credits

Chapter 1. p.6: watercolour by Dennis Rose, 1986. Courtesy, Confederation Life Gallery of Canadian History; pp.8-9: engravings by R.Petley, from Charles P. de Volpi's Nova Scotia = F1038 D49 Sp.Coll., Courtesy Special Collections, Dalhousie University Libraries; p.11: oil on canvas by Robert Field, ca.1815, collection and Courtesy of Art Gallery of Nova Scotia; p.13: oil on canvas by William Kitchin, 1822, collection of Art Gallery of Nova Scotia; p.14: Woolford, John E. Sketches in Nova Scotia for 1818 #44 and #46. Courtesy William Inglis Morse Collection, Special Collections Department, Dalhousie University Libraries; p.15: Woolford, J.E., 1817, Courtesy Nova Scotia Museum (N-8247); p.16: photo by author; p.17: Courtesy of Ken MacDonald; p.18 & 19: Watercolour, The Old School, by Janet McKean, 1932. Courtesy Public Archives of Nova Scotia (PANS): #1979-147.146, 42-11; p.20: PANS: Thomas McCulloch (People) and Places: Pictou: Houses: McCulloch, ca.1912; p.21: top: Courtesy of Kezia Matheson; bottom: Edward Mortimer: oil on Canvas by Robert Field, ca. 1815, collection of Art Gallery of Nova Scotia. Chapter 2. p.22: Ken MacDonald; p.23, top: photo of painting by and copyright to Miller Tibbetts, Courtesy of Mr. Tibbetts and Clifford MacPherson; right: Courtesy Pictou County Historical Society Museum; p.24, left: Courtesy Michael Sinclair; right: Photo by Shirley Locke, Courtesy Elsie and Dr. Howard Locke; p.25: Courtesy Don MacIssac; p.26 and 27: Clifford MacPherson; p.28: PANS: Pictou 1908: Pictou Lighthouse Album; p.29, left: Watercolours and gouache by William G.R. Hind, The Pictou Sketchbook #26A, #27B #39B. Art Gallery of Windsor; right: Waldren Collection, Dalhousie University Archives; bottom: Michael Sinclair; p.30: Engraving from Canadian Illustrated News, copying a photograph by J.R.P.Fraser, watercolour Courtesy Robert Hoegg; p.31: The Pictou Sketchbook #21A. Art Gallery of Windsor; p.32: PANS, Architectural Drawing, by Stirling, #1.3.3.1, n-423(2); p.33: PANS: Acc.#1487-82, Loc.#38-3; p.34: Burning Bush Museum, First Presbyterian Church, Pictou; p.35: Courtesy Raymond Gregory; p.36: Both Pictures, Courtesy Burning Bush Museum; p.37: Clifford MacPherson; p.38: Ken MacDonald; p.39: top and bottom left: Dr. Howard and Elsie Locke; bottom right: Ken MacDonald; p.40: Courtesy Henry Hayman; p.41: Watercolour of engraving from L'Opinion Publique, December 2, 1880. Property of the author; p.42: bottom photos, Courtesy William MacEachern; top: Courtesy, Murray Holley; p.43: top photos: William MacEachern; bottom, Courtesy Chesley "Ted" Fraser; p.44: Waldren Collection; p.45: top: William MacEachern; bottom: Waldren Collection; p.46: William MacEachern; p.47: top: Ken MacDonald; bottom: Courtesy Scotsburn Dairy; right: Print collection #250/ deVolpi's Nova Scotia = F1038 D49 Sp.Coll. Courtesy Charles P.deVolpi Collection, Special Collections Department, Dalhousie University Libraries; p.48: Courtesy Northumberland Fisheries Museum; p.49: Ken MacDonald; p.50: left, 2 photos: Ted Fraser; bottom: Ken MacDonald; right: Courtesy Dalhousie University Archives; p.51: Clifford

MacPherson; bottom: Kezia Matheson; p.52: top: PANS: Pictou 1908: Pictou Lighthouse Album; bottom: Waldren Collection; p.53: Courtesy Brian Cuthbertson, Department of Culture; p.54: top: Raymond Gregory; bottom: Waldren Collection; p.55: Waldren Collection; p.56: Ken MacDonald; p.57: both: Henry Hayman; p.58, 59, 60: Waldren collection; p.61: top: the author; bottom: Waldren Collection; p.62: Michael Sinclair; p.64: Pictou County Historical Society; p.65: top: Henry Hayman; bottom: William MacEachern; p.66: top: William MacEachern; middle: Courtesy Ida Lawrence; bottom: Pictou County Historical Society; p.67: both: Waldren Collection; p.68: Courtesy Ella Sangster; p.68-69: Dr. Howard and Elsie Locke; p70: Waldren Collection; p.71: top: Creighton collection; bottom: Ken MacDonald; pp.73-74: Waldren Collection; p.75: William MacEachern; p.76: top: Michael Sinclair; left: Waldren Collection; right: Ida Lawrence; p.77: top and bottom: Ken MacDonald: centre: Clifford MacPherson; p.78: top and bottom: Waldren Collection; centre: Ken MacDonald; p.79: Dr. Howard and Elsie Locke; p.80: both: Clifford MacPherson; p.81: Waldren Collection; p.82: Courtesy of Nova Scotia Museum of Industry; p.83: top, left: Miller Tibbetts painting, photo by Clifford MacPherson; right: Clifford MacPherson; p.84-85: William MacEachern; p.86: top right: Clifford MacPherson; bottom: Kezia Matheson; Centre: PANS, Bollinger collection #4817-12; top: Waldren Collection; p.87: Courtesy of Margaret Dickie MacDonald; bottom: Waldren Collection; p.88: both: Northumberland Fisheries Museum; p.89: Don MacIssac; p.90: top: Clifford MacPherson. ; bottom: Don MacIssac; pp.90-91: Waldren Collection; pp.92-93: Clifford MacPherson; p.93: bottom: Ken MacDonald; p.94: top: Henry Hayman; bottom: Waldren Collection; p.95: William MacEachern; p.96: PANS, New Glasgow 1933, Archimedes Street; p.97: William MacEachern; pp.98-99: Waldren Collection; p.100: Pictou County Historical Society; p.102: Waldren Collection; p.103: top: Ken MacDonald; left: the Author; right: William MacEachern; p.104: top: Pictou County Historical Society; bottom: Courtesy Catherine Clark; p.105: Waldren Collection; p.106: Clifford MacPherson; p.107: top: Courtesy Eric and Jean Williams; bottom: PANS, 1994-280, No. 129; p.108: Copyright and courtesy, Robert Chambers, loaned by N.S. Sport Heritage Centre; bottom: Waldren Collection; p.109: Copyright and Courtesy, Robert Chambers, print loaned by N.S. Sport Heritage Centre; bottom: Waldren Collection; p.110: left: Created by Sandy MacBeth, loaned by Clifford MacPherson; top: Waldren Collection; bottom: Courtesy J.B. Ferguson; p.112 - 113: William MacEachern; p.113: top: PANS: Places: New Glasgow: Car Works 1963; p.114: J.B. Ferguson; bottom: Sobeys; p.115: top: PANS, Clairtone Fonds 31-1-7, Clairtone #53; bottom: Government Services Collection, Box 10; p.116: top: Northumberland Fisheries Museum; bottom, left: Jensen sketch, Courtesy Clarence Porter; right: PANS, Government Services, Box 4; p.117: Scotsburn Co-operative Dairy; bottom: J.B. Ferguson; p.118: left: F.O. McLeod Photo, Courtesy and coypright of Robert Murray

Photography, loaned by Lois Tower; right: both Courtesy of John Soosar;
p.119: top: F.O. MacLeod Photo, Courtesy and copyright of Robert
Murray Photography, painted and loaned by Mabel Sinnis; bottom: PANS,
Government Services, Box 8; p.120: Courtesy of Sheila Robson; p.121:
Courtesy of Patricia Fraser Allen; p.122: Waldren Collection; right: Ida
Lawrence; p.123: top: Dept. of Tourism, courtesy of Graham Holman;
bottom: Courtesy of June and John Thompson; Ornamental pictures
thoughout text were photographed by Norman Munroe, and include rugs
from Cameron and Virginia Garrett; artifacts from the Nova Scotia
Museum of Industry; Mi'kmaq crafts from Jenny Stevens's MicMac
Country Shop and antiques and collectibles from Edward MacArthur's
Garretts'-by-the-Bridge.